EXTENDING

WordPe

Carol McKenzie
Pat Tidswell

HEINEMANN
EDUCATIONAL

Heinemann Educational,
a division of Heinemann Educational Books Ltd,
Halley Court, Jordan Hill, Oxford OX2 8EJ

OXFORD LONDON EDINBURGH
MADRID ATHENS BOLOGNA PARIS
MELBOURNE SYDNEY AUCKLAND SINGAPORE
TOKYO IBADAN NAIROBI HARARE
GABORONE PORTSMOUTH NH (USA)

First Published 1992

94 95 96 11 10 9 8 7 6 5

A catalogue record for this book is available from the British Library on request

ISBN 0 435 451170

Designed by Ken Vail Graphic Design, Cambridge
using Quark XPress™ 3.1 on the Apple Macintosh™ Ci

Printed in Great Britain by Thomson Litho, East Kilbride, Scotland

Acknowledgements
The authors and publishers would like to thank the RSA for permission to reproduce examination requirements and the list of standard abbreviations.

Contents

Extending WordPerfect has been written as a continuation text to *Introducing WordPerfect* * by the same authors. It has been designed as a progressive course and is suitable for use in the classroom, in an open learning workshop, or as a private study aid.

Extending WordPerfect will help those preparing to take an intermediate examination in Word Processing, using WordPerfect Versions 5.0 or 5.1. However, the book would be equally useful to those who use WordPerfect and simply wish to extend their working knowledge.

Previous experience

It is assumed that you have completed an elementary (Stage I) word processing course, using WordPerfect, and are therefore familiar with conventional document layout and basic text processing principles and practice. It is also assumed that you are familiar with the most commonly used WordPerfect commands as outlined in the previous book, *Introducing WordPerfect*.

Format

Full instructions for the commands and functions required in the preparation of particular documents are given at the beginning of each unit, followed by practice exercises.
Consolidation practice is available after Units 3 and 6, i.e. after all the topics for each part of each syllabus have been covered.
Print-out checks are included in the book and these may be used by both students and teachers.
Handy tips are included throughout the text to suggest ways in which functions can be carried out more quickly, easily or effectively.
A **glossary of WordPerfect commands** is available for quick reference at the back of the book.

Coverage

This book is designed for those of you preparing to take the **RSA Stage II Word Processing** examination, using WordPerfect Versions 5.0 or 5.1.
Units 1, 2 and 3 cover Part 1 of the Stage II examination.
Units 4, 5 and 6 cover Part 2 of the Stage II examination.
Consolidation work is included after Units 3 and 6.

Assessment

At the end of Unit 3 you should be able to do an RSA Stage II Part 1 paper:

(a) within a *one-and-a-quarter-hour* time limit
(b) with no more than eight accuracy and five presentation errors for a *Pass*
(c) with no more than three accuracy and three presentation errors for a *Distinction*

At the end of Unit 6 you should be able to do an RSA Stage II Part 2 paper:

(a) within a *one-and-a-quarter-hour* time limit
(b) with no more than four accuracy and three presentation errors for a *Pass*
(c) with no more than two accuracy and two presentation errors for a *Distinction*

* This publication covers the following syllabuses:
RSA Computer Literacy and Information Technology (word processing application)
RSA Core Text Processing Skills (taken on a word processor)
RSA Stage I Word Processing

Using on-screen menus in WordPerfect 5.1

WordPerfect 5.1 offers the facility of drop-down on-screen menus which may be used by either keyboard or mouse-driven operation, in addition to, or instead of, the function keys. Instructions to access the on-screen menus, where relevant, have been included throughout the text. The appropriate mouse commands appear in boxes to the left of the page and the keyboard commands to which they relate have been highlighted for easy identification. From this point operators may choose whether to use the mouse or the keyboard.

The menu bar appears at the top of the screen as follows:

```
File | Edit | Search | Layout | Mark | Tools | Font | Graphics | Help
```

The initial one-line menu bar may be permanently displayed on screen by choosing the appropriate options under the **Shift+F1** (Setup) key.

To select an option from the on-screen menu – keyboard operation

Press: **Alt**
Type: the highlighted letter of the option required

– mouse operation

Move the mouse pointer to the option required and click the mouse button

A drop-down menu will appear on screen:

```
File | Edit | Search | Layout | Mark | Tools | Font | Graphics | Help

    [Move (Cut)          ]
    [Copy                ]
    [Paste               ]
    [Append              ]
    ----------------------
    [Delete              ]
    [Undelete            ]
    ----------------------
    [Block               ]
    [Select              ]
    [Comment             ]
    [Convert Case        ]
    [Protect Block       ]
    ----------------------
    [Switch Document     ]
    [Window              ]
    ----------------------
    [Reveal Codes        ]
```

To exit from the on-screen menu without making a selection – keyboard operation

Press: **F7** (Exit) or **F1** (Cancel)

– mouse operation

Position the mouse pointer anywhere on screen *outside* the menu box and click the mouse button.

One of WordPerfect's most useful features is the **help** key. If you forget, or haven't learned, how to carry out a particular function you can use the help feature for guidance. Pressing **F3** (the help key) temporarily replaces your normal editing screen with the initial help screen. You may then:

- Either press any letter to get an alphabetical list of features and the name of the key which will activate that feature, for example typing **M** will bring up a list of all the features that begin with the letter M as shown below:

Key	Feature	Key Name
Ctrl-PgUp	Macro Commands	Macro Commands
Ctrl-F10	Macro Commands, Help on	Macro Definition
Ctrl-F10	Macro, Define	Macro Define
Ctrl-F10	Macro Editor	Ctrl-F10, Edit
Alt-F10	Macro, Execute	Macro
Shift-F1	Main Dictionary(s)	Setup,7
Shft-F8	Manual Hyphenation	Format,1
Shft-Tab	Margin Release	Shft-Tab

For more information on a function press the function key itself.

- Or press **F3** again to bring up the help template which displays all the features and function keys at a glance:

	Shell	Spell	
F1	SETUP	<-SEARCH	F2
	Thesaurus	Replace	
	Cancel	Search->	
	Screen	Move	
F3	SWITCH	->INDENT<-	F4
	Reveal Codes	Block	
	Help	->Indent	
	Text In/Out	Tab Align	
F5	DATE/OUTLINE	CENTRE	F6
	Mark Text	Flush Right	
	List Files	Bold	
	Footnote	Font	
F7	PRINT	FORMAT	F8
	Maths/Columns	Style	
	Exit	Underline	
	Merge Sort	Macro Def.	
F9	MERGE CODES	RETRIEVE	F10
	Graphics	Macro	
	Merge R	Save	

Legend:
Ctrl + Function Key
SHIFT + FUNCTION KEY
Alt + Function Key
Function key alone

To leave help

Press: the space bar or ↵.

If you are preparing for an examination, you are advised to work through the book unit by unit.

The book has been planned as a progressive course and some of the work you will do in the later units is based on text you keyed in earlier.

Do not delete files from your disk – you will need them later!

Working through a unit

1  *When you see this symbol read all the information* before you begin. You may also need to refer back to this information as you carry out the exercises.

2  *When you see this symbol carry out the exercises, following the numbered steps*, e.g. 1.1, 1.2.

3 Use WordPerfect's **Spellcheck** facility to check your document.

4 *Proofread* your work carefully – Spellcheck doesn't find every error.

5 Use WordPerfect's **View** facility to check that your document is going to be correct when it is printed. This is particularly useful when you need to check headers, page numbering and justification as these features do not show on the normal working screen.

6 *Save your work* on to your floppy disk (usually in A drive) and *clear the screen*.

7 *Call up the directory* (List Files) of your disk on to the screen and *print your work* from this directory. (Although you may, of course, print your work direct from the screen, it is good practice, particularly if you are preparing for an examination, to print from the list of files.)

8 Compare your work with the *print-out checks* at the back of the book. (If you are using this book in class, your tutor may wish to check your work.)

9 Exit WordPerfect or begin next unit (as appropriate).

General hints

It is easy to think that because you have used the **Spellcheck** facility on your word processing system, your work is accurate. Automatic spell checking is very useful and you should always 'run Spellcheck' before you save or print a document, but you must *also* proofread the document yourself.

The Spellcheck facility simply compares each word you have keyed in with its own 'dictionary' of words.

Candidates who fail examinations often do so because their proofreading is not adequate. One of the most common errors is the omission of words. Unfortunately, if you have missed out some words, or not deleted some words as instructed, spellchecking will not detect this.

If you have typed the wrong 'version' of a word, e.g. 'there' instead of 'their', spellchecking will not detect this as both versions are spelled correctly.

Only *you* can tell if you have copied names of people or places correctly and if a piece of information you were asked to find is accurate.

For example, Spellcheck cannot tell if the date you have keyed in for Thursday of next week is the correct one. Don't guess – use a diary or calendar.

The skills of proofreading are essential in text processing. You should train yourself to check every detail in any work you have done ***before*** you print it so as not to waste paper. It is not enough to check the work on your screen, you must ***compare*** it with the 'copy' from which you are working – going through it word by word.

1.1 Switch on and load WordPerfect.

1.2 Insert your work disk in the disk drive.

Check that WordPerfect is set up to save your work to the appropriate drive (usually Drive A).

1.3 Exercise 1a.

Proofread the following text as instructed.

There are 12 errors.

When you have identified all the errors key in a correct copy and check against the original manuscript. Make any necessary amendments.

Never forget to type your name and the exercise number on line 1.

Our new junior has made lots of errors!

Please key in a correct copy from the typescript below. Use the manuscript to check that your work is better. Retain justified margin.

bold → CALDERGHYLL (REF CMB422)

This mid-terraced house is near the centre of hte town and covenient for allamenities. Luxuriously furnished with antiques and equipped with every every labour-saving device, this house offers the the ideal place for a relaxing break. Acommodation is for 4 people in 2 twin-bedded rooms on the first floor. The ground floor comprises lounge, kitchen and dinning room. The first flor bathroom has both bath and shower.
The owner does not object to one samll dog kept under proper controle. [PRICE BAND 12.

NB Available from (1st Sat of next month)

CALDERGHYLL (REF CMB424)

This mid-terraced house is near the centre of the town and convenient for all amenities. Luxuriously furnished with antiques and equipped with every labour-saving device, this house offers the ideal place for a relaxing break. Accommodation is for 4 people in 2 twin-bedded rooms on the first floor. The ground floor comprises lounge, kitchen, and dining room. The first floor bathroom has both bath and shower. [The owner does not object to one small dog kept under proper control. [PRICE BAND 12. NB Available from ——.

Printing from the List Files screen

When you are preparing for an examination, you should get into the habit of printing from the List Files (directory) screen and not from the document itself.

File
List Files

1. Save your work using the filename given.
2. Clear the screen.
3. Press: **F5** ↵
4. Move the cursor to highlight the file you wish to print.
5. Press: **4** (*Print*)
6. Press: ↵ **on (All)** if you wish to print all the pages in the document
   Press: **1** ↵ if you wish to print only page 1. (Key in the appropriate numbers to print the pages you require.)

Save and print a copy of your work. Use the filename **EX1A**.

Check your work against the print-out check on page 64.

Handy tip

Justified right margin check

In WordPerfect the right justification does not show on screen. Remember to use the view facility to check your document.

Handy tip

Changing the unit of measurement

File
Setup
Environment
Units of Measure

If your status line shows the line and position indicators in inches, you can change the display. The line display can be changed to tell you which line you are on and the position display can be changed to show the column position in pitch.

Press: **Shift+F1** (Set-up key)
Press: **8** (Units of measure)
Press: **1** (Display)
Type: **u** (WordPerfect units lines/columns)
Press: **2** (Status line display)
Type: **u** (WordPerfect units lines/columns)
Press: **F7** (Exit)

Changing the line length

Layout
Line

You may be asked to change the 'line length' of a document to a fixed number of characters. This is achieved either by *indenting* (**F4** key) or *insetting the margins* (**Shift + F8** Format menu).

(It is not always possible in word processing to be completely accurate in this respect and examiners should be aware of this and be lenient in their marking of this feature.)

The width of A4 paper is approximately 8.2 in (*or 82 characters in 10 pitch*). The 'default' margins in WordPerfect are set at 1 in (*or 10 characters in 10 pitch*) at each side. Therefore, in WordPerfect, there are 62 characters across a normal typing line.

The extra characters to be added to the margins to reduce the typing line can be incorporated in any of the following three ways:

1. all the required extra characters added to the left margin, or
2. all the required extra characters added to the right margin, or
3. some of the extra characters added to the right margin and some to the left margin (*these amounts do not have to be equal*).

Examples

Layout
Line

To change the line length to 50 characters, you need to increase the margins by 12 characters: you could use the Format menu (**Shift** + **F8**) to add 12 characters to the left margin, or to add 12 characters to the right margin, or to add 6 characters to each margin.

To change the line length to 52 characters, you need to increase the margins by 10 characters: you could use the Indent key (**Shift** + **F4**) *once* to indent the text by 5 spaces at each side, or you could use **F4** on its own *twice* to indent the text by 10 spaces at the left.

1.4 **Exercise 1b.**

Proofread the following text as instructed.

When you have identified all the errors, key in a correct copy and check against the original manuscript. *Change the line length to 50 characters.*

Make any necessary amendments.

Save and print a copy of your work. Use the filename **EX1B**.

Check your work against the print-out check on page 64.

My daughter kindly offered to do this on her computer at home. As you can see, it is not perfect! Please produce a correct copy, using a justified right margin.

tHere is no reason why youshould not by overdue products becuase the shopkeeper is obliged to provide goods which meet a certain quality - they must not be "bad or "off". Even if you buy such goods at a reduced price, your legal rights is not affected. If you are unable to obtain staisfaction from the shop manager, contact the local Trading Standards Officer thro' the town Hall.

Most food producers need to maintin a good reputation and and they will usually take any compliant very seriously indeed. It is often a good idea to write to Managing Director of an organisatoin enclosing, if poss, a sample of the defective goods. You may have your costes refunded and sometimes a free gift or sample is sent to you as a token of goodwill.

T S Orwen (1st Friday of next month)

bold

There is no reason why you should not buy overdue products because the shopkeeper is obliged to provide goods which meet a certain quality – they must not be "bad" or "off". Even if you buy such goods at a reduced price, your legal rights are not affected. If you are unable to obtain satisfaction from the shop manager, contact the local Trading Standards Officer through the Town Hall.

Most food producers need to maintain a good reputation and they will usually take any complaint very seriously indeed. It is often a good idea to write to the Managing Director of an organisation enclosing, if possible, a sample of the defective goods. You may have your costs refunded and sometimes a free gift or sample is sent to you as a token of goodwill.

(TS Orwen (1st Friday of next month))

↗ embolden please

Consistency of presentation

You should always be consistent in the way in which you present information within a document.

Abbreviations used to indicate measurements, weights, times, money

Be consistent in the use of an abbreviation to represent a measurement or a weight, such as mm, cm, ft, in, kg, oz, lb.

For example, don't key in 30" in one place and 24 in somewhere else in the document. Be consistent – use either " or in but *not a mixture of the two.*

You may leave one space before the abbreviation or no spaces but you must be consistent.

For example, don't key in 46kg in one place and 46 kg somewhere else in the document.

Stick to the 12-hour clock or the 24-hour clock when using times.

Be consistent in the use of pm, o'clock, hrs.

For example, don't key in 1600 hrs in one place and 7.30 am somewhere else in the document.

When using an abbreviation for currency (e.g. $, DM, FF) stick to one method of presentation.

For example, don't key in £15 in one place and £12.50 somewhere else in the document. Both amounts should show the pence – £15.00 and £12.50. Don't key in FF100 in one place and 100 French francs somewhere else in the document.

You should use either £ or p but *not both together in one amount* – £0.50p is wrong.

Handy tip

'Hard' spaces between words

Sometimes it is desirable to keep two words or symbols together rather than having them separated by the wrap-round function.

For example, reading is made more difficult if **25 mm** is split as it is in this sentence, and also **Mr Nettleton** would be better all on one line.

To avoid this (using the above example):

Type: **25**
Press: **Home**
Press: **Spacebar**
Type: **mm**

25 mm will be kept together either at the end of the first line or at the beginning of the second line.

Words and figures

You should be consistent in the way you present numbers within a document.

For example, don't key in 40 miles in one place and fifty-five miles somewhere else in the document.

Look through the text first and decide on words or figures. Think about these two examples:

- 1,234,650 is difficult to express in words
- 1 looks strange as the first word of a sentence.

Other possible inconsistencies

You should be consistent in using the dash (–) or the hyphen (-) between words and symbols. *The keyboard symbol is the same; the spacing on either side of the symbol is different.*

For example, don't key in 4 – 6 in one place and 16–21 somewhere else in the document. Also, don't key in 4 to 6 in one place and 16–21 somewhere else in the document.

The word 'to' can also be used in this way.

For example, 3 to 4 weeks' time, Tuesday to Thursday. Don't key in Friday – Sunday in one place and Monday to Wednesday somewhere else in the document.

You should be consistent in keying-in words that can be spelt in two different ways.

For example, don't type 'organise' in one place and 'organize' somewhere else in the document.

You should be consistent in the amount of space you leave after punctuation.

For example, don't leave one space after a full stop in one place and two spaces after a full stop somewhere else in the document.

You should standardize the layout of any document you are producing.

For example, don't mix paragraph styles, and make all headings the same style.

Headers and footers

A **header** is a piece of text in the form of a title, heading, or reference which appears at the top of all pages of a multi-page document. A **footer** is the same kind of text appearing at the bottom of all pages.

WordPerfect allows you to 'set' the headers and footers by keying in the text only once. The header or footer will then automatically appear on all pages.

Note: The header/footer text does not show on the screen but you can check that it is present by using the **View** function within the print menu.

To set headers on every page of a document

Layout
Page

1 Position cursor at top of document by pressing **Home-Home-↑** (The header *must* be set on line 1.)

2 Press: **Shift + F8** (Format menu)

3 Select: **2** (Format Page menu)

4 Select: **3** (Headers)

5 Select: **1** (Header A)

6 Select: **2** (Every Page) (A blank screen appears for you to type the header text.)

Layout Justify Centre
Layout Justify Full

Font Appearance Bold
Underline

7 Type: **the header text**
You can centre the header (**Shift + F6**)
You can justify the header (**Alt + F6**)
You can use **bold** or **underline** for the header if requested.

8 Press: **F7** twice (to exit the header)

Note: if you are producing multi-page documents in an examination you can save time by using the header function so that your name, centre number and task number appear on every page.

To do this: key in your name and other details as the first line of the header, then leave a blank line before keying in the requested header text.

To set footers on every page of a document

Follow the instructions given above for headers, selecting **footers** at the Format Page menu.

To edit headers and footers

After selecting Header A or Footer A

Select: **5** (Edit)

Make the necessary formatting changes

Press: **F7** (Exit)

Edit
Reveal Codes

Handy tip

Headers not showing in view mode

If you find that when you view your document the headers are not shown, you may need to check that the header command is the *first* command on your document. Use reveal codes (**F11** or **Alt + F3**). You may have to delete the header codes and re-set the header in the correct position (first making sure that the cursor is at the very top of your document by pressing **Home-Home-↑**).

Page numbering

It is often necessary for the pages of a document to be numbered. WordPerfect allows you to 'set' the page numbering by giving the commands once only. Consecutive page numbers will then appear automatically on all pages.

Note: page numbers do not show on the screen but you can check that they are present by using the **View** function within the print menu.

To set page numbering on every page of a document

Layout
Page

1 Position cursor at top of document (after any header code)
2 Press: **Shift + F8** (Format menu)
3 Select: **2** (Format Page menu)
4 Select: **7** (Page Numbering) (Version 5.0) *or*
Select: **6** (Page Numbering)
Select: **4** (Page Number Position) (Version 5.1)
(You are presented with choices of frequency and position of page numbers)
5 Select: the number corresponding to the position required (for letters, select a position at the foot of the page)
6 Press: **F7** (to exit)
7 Press: **F7** (to get back to your document)

Page numbering on letters

It is usual to omit the page number on the first page of a letter. WordPerfect allows you to set page numbering and then to suppress this facility on any given page.

Suppression of page numbering

To suppress page numbering on the current page the cursor must be positioned on the page where the suppression is to take place when the commands for this facility are given.

The suppression should be carried out after step 6 in the page numbering sequence at the Format Page menu screen.

1 Press: **9** (Suppress this page only) (Version 5.0) *or*
Press: **8** (Suppress this page only) (Version 5.1)
2 Press: **4** (Suppress page numbering)
3 Type: **Y** (for *Yes*)
4 Press: **F7** (to get back to your document)

Note: It is also possible to suppress headers and footers by the same method.

Pagination (page breaks) in multi-page documents

Page breaks (new pages) should be inserted in sensible places within a document so that the document is easy to read.

WordPerfect automatically makes 'soft' page breaks when the number of lines on a page has been exceeded, but sometimes this break is not in a satisfactory position. A soft page break is shown by a single line of dashes across the screen:

- -

You can insert your own 'hard' page break by pressing **Ctrl** + ↵

A hard page break is shown by a double line of dashes across the screen:

==

In the Reveal Codes mode a soft page break is shown by (**SPg**) and a hard page break by (**HPg**).

Pagination in business letters

Consider the following points when paginating a business letter.

1. The complimentary close of a letter (Yours ..... etc.) should never be the *only* text on the last page. Ideally, there should be at least three or four lines of text above the complimentary close.
2. You should not divide a word between one page and the next.
3. You should not leave only the first line of a paragraph at the bottom of a page (a 'widow').
4. You should not carry forward only the last line of a paragraph on to the next page (an 'orphan').

Handy tip

Preventing widows and orphans

WordPerfect can automatically ensure that you do not have widows and orphans in your document. Widow lines will be moved to the next page. Orphan lines will have the previous line of text carried on to the next page to make a two-line block.

To set widow/orphan protection:

Layout
Line

1. Position cursor at top of document
2. Press: **Shift** + **F8** (Format menu)
3. Select: **1** (Line Format menu)
4. Select: **9** (Widow/orphan protection)
5. Type: **Y** (for Yes)
6. Press: **F7** (to exit)

In the following two exercises you will key in a letter from manuscript copy. The letter will go on to two pages and you will be required to put into practice all the functions and techniques described on pages 10–14.

You will retrieve the text you previously keyed in and saved in Unit 1. Follow instructions 2.1 to 2.11 step by step, in the order given.

2.1 **Exercise 2a.** Starting with a clear screen, set a one-line *header* to show:
Your name Exercise 2A

2.2 Set *page numbering*, selecting a position for the number at the foot of the page, suppressing the page number on page 1.

2.3 *Key in the letter* from manuscript, ensuring that you expand abbreviations and use a consistent style of presentation and layout.

2.4 At the * sign *retrieve the text* that you saved as **EX1A** into the current document.

2.5 Use the *Reveal Codes* mode to *remove the justification* on the recalled text.

2.6 *Key in* the remainder of the letter.

2.7 Spellcheck your letter.

2.8 Proofread your letter, comparing it carefully with the manuscript.

2.9 Paginate your letter by inserting a hard page break in a suitable place.

2.10 View your letter to make sure that the header and page numbering is present.

2.11 Save and print a copy of your work. Use the filename **EX2A**.

Exercise 2a. Please key in the letter, retrieving text from disk where indicated. Use a ragged right margin throughout and standardise the layout. Save and print your work. Use the filename EX2A.

Ref EWP/2A

Please mark URGENT

Mrs B S Kelly
236 Main Street
Weston
BARNSLEY
BY10 8JJ

Dr Mrs K ______

Cumbrian Cottages ← (Caps & underline)

Thank you for yr letter of (last Monday's date) requesting info on self-catering cottages in Cumbria. I have pleasure in setting out below details of the accom at "Calderghyll" wh is available ^ wh you mentioned. (for the dates)

A ~~reservation~~ booking form is enclosed for yr use & I hope that you wl find that you are satisfied w "C ____" from the details shown. At this time of yr many people are making holiday arrangements & I wd suggest that you telephone our bookings ~~section~~ dept ✓ on 061-763205 asap in order to make a ^ reservation. (provisional)

You can telephone, at any time between 8 am and 7.00 pm from Mon to Fri and between 1000 hrs and 5 pm from Sat – Sun.

* (Retrieve details of Calderghyll saved as EX1A and insert here)

I wd like to take this opp of assuring you of the high standards of service ^ from our org. (wh you can expect)

We pride ourselves on the careful and thorough processing of (bookings) & (enquiries). All of our properties are regularly inspected & members of staff are available at ~~all~~ any time to solve any problems wh may arise.

[Please contact me if you wd like any further info or advice. I look forward to hearing from you in the near future.]

[We recom that you take advantage of our inexpensive insurance ^ cover. The cost is competitive at £4.50 per person per week, and 15 pounds for a family (4–6 persons).]

Yrs scly

Elisabeth W Pendragon
(RURAL IDYLLS PLC)

Abbreviations

There are additional abbreviations for the Stage II examination. The abbreviations are not followed by a full stop as they were in Stage I. A complete list is given below:

accom	accommodation	misc	miscellaneous
a/c (s)	account(s)	necy	necessary
ack	acknowledge	opp(s)	opportunity/ies
advert(s)	advertisement(s)	org	organisation
altho'	although	p/t	part-time
appt(s)	appointment(s)	poss	possible
approx	approximately	rec(s)	receipt(s)
asap	as soon as possible	rec	receive
bel	believe	recd	received
bus	business	recom	recommend
cat(s)	catalogue(s)	ref(s)	reference(s)
cttee(s)	committee(s)	refd	referred
co(s)	company/ies	resp	responsible
def	definitely	sec(s)	secretary/ies
dev	develop	sep	separate
dr	dear	sh	shall
ex	exercise	shd	should
exp(s)	expense(s)	sig(s)	signatures
exp	experience	suff	sufficient
f/t	full-time	temp	temporary
gov(s)	government(s)	thro'	through
gntee(s)	guarantee(s)	wh	which
hrs	hours	wd	would
immed	immediately	w	with
incon	inconvenient/ence	wl	will
info	information	yr(s)	year(s)
mfr(s)	manufacturer(s)	yr(s)	your(s)

Days of the week:		*Months of the year*:	
Mon	Monday	Jan	January
Tues	Tuesday	Feb	February
Wed	Wednesday	Mar	March

Words in address:		*Complimentary close*:	
Cres	Crescent	ffly	faithfully
Dr	Drive	scly	sincerely
Rd	Road		

Note: you should *retain* other commonly used abbreviations such as etc, e.g., NB, & (in company names – *not* & in text).

You may *not* take the above lists with you into the examination – so you need to learn them. However, don't forget that you are allowed to use WordPerfect's Spellcheck facility and, of course, you may use a dictionary.

2.12 **Exercise 2b.**

Key in the following letter, incorporating the text you produced in **EX1B** at the point shown.

Follow the same procedures in the same order as for Exercise 2a by following steps 2.1 to 2.11.

Save and print a copy of your work. Use the filename **EX2B**.

Ref TSO/WP/2B — FOR THE ATTENTION OF MS W GOOD
The Consumer Guide
172-175 Byre Street
YORK YO2 1JM

Dr Sirs/~~Madam~~

(LETTERS PAGE) — emphasise

I recently received a request from yr org for a contribution to yr Consumer Info column, wh I have pleasure in setting out below.

(Not at its best?) ← caps + bold
(*There is no reason . . . (ex1B))
Indent ½" at left only.

It is poss that you are already aware of the fact that it is not unknown for ~~some~~ certain people to take advantage of a mfr's generosity by frequently returning 'faulty' ~~products~~. ~~goods~~ (✓) Most mfrs keep records of these transactions so it is not a practice wh I wd recom and it involves more ~~than~~ (effort) and (time) than it is worth.

Altho' there is considerable exp. in postage, some people have almost made a p/t job out of this ~~pastime~~ hobby!

Do you think that an extra paragraph to this effect wd be useful ^ for yr readers? (or relevant)

FOOD ADDITIVES
I hope to hear from you asap on my article on ~~food~~ additives as you said you may be interested in this.

Please let me know ~~what you think~~ yr decision both on the (text) (submitted) and the additional info ~~paragraph~~.

I enclose my bus card so that you may telephone me. I am in f/t employment so you can reach me between the hours of 9.00 am & 1700 hrs at my bus number. After 6 pm I can be contacted at home.

Yrs ffly

T S O____ (Mr)

Page breaks within a multi-page document

Sometimes you are asked to 'leave page breaks' or 'retain page breaks' as shown on the copy document. (*Watch out for this instruction in an examination.*)

Sometimes you are expected to *use your own judgement* as to the most suitable position(s) for new pages to begin.

Layout
Page

If you cannot fit all the text you require on a certain page, decrease the size of the bottom margin to ½ in or less if necessary – it is usually defaulted to 1 in. Use the **Shift** + **F8** Format menu to do this.

Look back at the notes on page 14 of Unit 2 to remind yourself of the 'rules' on pagination.

Formatting requirements for multi-page documents

You will be expected to make the following formatting changes in the RSA Stage II Part 1 examination:

Leaving clear line spaces (e.g. for photograph)

Remember there are 6 lines to 1 in: to leave 1 in clear you must leave 6 clear lines.

Insetting margins (Shift + F8 Format menu)

Remember there are 10 characters to 1 in in 10 pitch.

Indenting text (F4 indent key)

Remember that **F4** indents by $\frac{1}{2}$ in from left **Shift** + **F4** indents by $\frac{1}{2}$ in at left *and* right, using default tab stops.

Moving blocks of text and copying blocks of text (F12 (Alt + F4) and Ctrl + F4)

Read the instructions carefully – don't confuse the terms 'move' and 'copy'.

Move a block means that the text appears in only 1 place – you simply have to reposition the block.

Copy a block means that the text appears in 2 (or more) places – you leave the block in its original position *and* put an identical copy of it in another position.

If you 'move' a block instead of 'copy' a block in an examination you will get a lot of accuracy errors, as every missing word counts as 1 error!

Organizing text editing in a multi-page document

When a document runs into several pages and there are many changes to be made you may sometimes feel that you have become 'lost', particularly if you have been distracted.

The following is a *suggested* method of working that you might like to adopt. Using this method means that you will return to the top of the document and work through it several times, carrying out a different function each time. This might seem time-consuming but if you always use the method you will get into a routine and you will be sure that you have not missed out anything.

There is an added advantage in going through a document several times – you might spot an error that can be corrected as you scan through the work!

After setting headers and page numbering and viewing to check that they are correct:

1. Carry out all the necessary **text amendments**, e.g. inserting or deleting of text *throughout the whole document*.
2. **Move blocks of text** and **copy blocks of text** as requested *throughout the whole document*.
3. **Search and replace** as requested.
4. **Allocate space** (*clear line spaces*) and **indent** or **inset margins** as requested.
5. **Paginate** your document as requested or as you think fit (*read the instructions*).
6. **Spellcheck** the whole document.
7. **Proofread** the whole document, comparing it word for word with the copy.
8. **View** your document to make sure that it is going to be printed correctly.
9. And finally **print** your work.

Handy tip

Case conversion

WordPerfect can change a block of text from upper case (capital letters) to lower case (small letters):

1 Shade the block of text to be changed using **F12** or **Alt** + **F4**
2 Press: **Shift** + **F3** (switch)
3 Select **1** (for upper case)
or **2** (for lower case)

Edit
ConWert
Case
To Upper
or
To Lower

Moving around the document – advanced methods

When you are checking and proofreading a multi-page document you need to be able to move the cursor quickly from one section to another.

Move cursor to end of current line

Press: **End**

Move cursor to top or bottom of current screen

Press: **Home ↑** or **Home ↓**

Move cursor to left or right of current screen

Press: **Home ←** or **Home →**

Move cursor to the top of previous page or top of next page

Press: **PgUp** or **PgDn**

Move cursor to the beginning or end of current document

Press: **Home Home ↑** or **Home Home ↓**
(**Home Home Home ↑** positions cursor *before* all formatting codes.)

Move cursor to specified page (sometimes called GoTo key)

Press: **Ctrl+Home**
Type: Number of page required at 'Go to'
Press: ↵

('Repositioning' appears at bottom left of screen and specified page appears on screen.)

Deleting text – advanced methods

To delete word to left of cursor

Press: **Home** + **← Del**

To delete word to right of cursor

Press: **Home** + **Del**

To delete from cursor to end of current line

Press: **Ctrl** + **End**

To delete from cursor to end of sentence

Press: **F12** (or **Alt** + **F4**) (to shade block)
Press: **.** (full stop) (shades to end of sentence)
Press: **Del** (delete key)
Press: **Y** (at '**Delete block Y/N?**')

To delete from cursor to end of page

Press: **Ctrl** + **PgDn**
Press: **Y** (at '**Delete Remainder of Page Y/N?**')

Don't forget – you can restore deleted text

Press: **F1**
Press: **1** (to restore block just deleted)
Press: **2** (to restore next to last deletion)

Handy tip

Shift + F3 – Doc 2

If your screen suddenly goes blank and you notice that **Doc 2** is showing on the status line, you may have pressed **Shift** + **F3** by mistake. To get back to your work, press **Shift** + **F3** again.

You are going to work on the text you created and saved as **EX2A**, but *before* you retrieve the document set the format (headers, page numbering, etc) by following steps 3.1 to 3.4 below.

3.1 **Exercise 3a.** Starting with a clear screen, set a three-line header as follows:

Name	Exercise 3A	(line 1)
(leave one clear line here)		(line 2)
RURAL IDYLLS		(line 3)

Note: use the header function in this way when practising examination work to ensure that your name, centre number and task number appear on every page printed.

In 'real life', of course, your name would not be required on a document.

3.2 Set page numbering to appear at the *bottom left* of every page.

3.3 View your document to check that the headers and page numbering are present.

3.4 You may choose whether to use a ragged or a justified right margin – set the format according to your choice.

3.5 Retrieve your file **EX2A**. At the Reveal Codes screen, delete the codes for page numbering and page number suppression.

3.6 Delete the reference, date, name and address and salutation from the letter.

3.7 Delete the complimentary close (Yours sincerely … Enc).

3.8 Amend the text in Exercise 3a as shown, inserting hard page break markers to place the text on three pages as shown.

Use the 'advanced methods' described to delete text as requested in the exercise.

Refer to the glossary to remind yourself about:

- *insetting text* (by changing margin settings), and
- *indenting text* (using **F4** Indent key).

Single line spacing please. Keep page breaks as shown.

CUMBRIAN COTTAGES — spaced caps, centre, no underline

underline as heading

~~Thank you for your letter of (correct date inserted for last Monday) requesting information on~~ Self-catering cottages in Cumbria. ~~I have pleasure in setting out below details of the accommodation at Calderghyll which is available for the dates which you mentioned~~.

~~A booking form is enclosed for your use and I hope that you will find that you are satisfied with Calderghyll from the details shown~~. At this time of year many people are making holiday arrangements. ~~and I would suggest that you~~ Telephone our bookings section on 061-763205 as soon as possible in order to make a provisional reservation. [You can telephone at any time between 8.00 am and 7.00 pm from Monday to Friday and between 9am ~~10.00 am~~ and 5.00 pm from Saturday to Sunday.

change times to 24-hr clock

*

[The Calderbrook area has two houses wh. are available within the dates required.]

indent ½" from left and right margins and change to CAPS

Make heading same style as 'Self-catering' on Page 1

CALDERGHYLL (REF CMB424) Leave 12 clear lines

This mid-terraced house is near the centre of ~~the town~~ Calderbrook and convenient for all amenities. Luxuriously furnished with antiques and equipped with every labour-saving device, this house offers the ideal place for a relaxing break.
Accommodation is for 4 people in 2 twin-bedded rooms on the first floor. The ground floor comprises lounge, kitchen and dining room. The first floor bathroom has both bath and shower.

The owner does not object to one small dog kept under proper control. Copy to Page 3 in same position under Brockholes.

PRICE BAND 12 NB Available from (correct date inserted for 1st Saturday of next month).

You can be assured ~~I would like to take this opportunity of assuring you~~ of ~~the~~ high standards of service ~~which you can expect~~ from our organisation.

We pride ourselves on the careful and thorough processing of enquiries and bookings. All of our properties are regularly inspected and members of staff are available at any time to solve any problems which may arise.

We recommend that you take advantage of our inexpensive insurance cover. The cost is competitive at £4.50 per person per week, and £15.00 for a family (4 to 6 persons).

Move to Page 1 and insert at *

Double spacing for these paras please.

(Standardise/shoulder headings throughout)

~~Please contact me if you would like any further information or advice. I look forward to hearing from you in the near future.~~

BROCK HOLES COTTAGE (REF CMB 546)

(please leave 15 clear lines for sketch)

This attractive stone cottage ~~is being~~ has been renovated to a very high standard.

It is particularly well-equipped, having an automatic washer, tumble drier, dishwasher & microwave oven.

Accom is ~~for~~ 3 or four persons in two bedrooms (one twin, one double). There is a comfortable ~~sitting room~~ lounge w a log fire & a sep kitchen/diner. The modern bathroom has a 3-piece suite and there is a sep. shower room on the ground floor. ✓

The property has the advantages of:

oil-fired central heating
electricity for cooking
private walled garden
garage for one car

← Inset by 6 spaces from left

(Copy sentence about dog here)

The cottage is one mile from shops & pub, and many clients have already made bookings.

[PRICE B — 10. NB Available from (2nd Sat of next month).

Use the advanced methods described to move the cursor around the document as you check, proofread and edit Exercise 3a.

3.9 Check that the hard page break markers are in the correct places on your document.

3.10 Spellcheck your document.

3.11 Proofread your document, comparing it very carefully with the copy.

Refer to the notes on consistency of presentation on pages 10–11 and *check that you have no inconsistencies* in your work.

3.12 View your document to make sure that the header and page numbering are present.

3.13 Save your work as **EX3A** *but do not print* your work until you have carried out the global search and replace function in step 3.14.

Do not move on to step 3.14 until you have read about global search and replace.

3.14 The word 'bookings' is to be replaced wherever it occurs in Exercise 3a with the word 'reservations'.

Use the global search and replace function to perform this task.

3.15 Save and print a copy of your work, replacing the old version of **EX3A** with the new version.

> ***Handy tip***
>
> To *search* through a portion of text instead of the whole document: use the **F12** or **Alt** + **F4** keys to block the portion of text you want to search through, then continue with the normal search procedure.

Global search and replace

WordPerfect can automatically find a given word and exchange it for another given word throughout a document. An example of the way in which this function could be used is a letter being sent out from a school to parents. It would be very easy to produce some letters that referred to 'your son' and some that referred to 'your daughter', or every occurrence of 'he' could be changed to 'she'.

You can use WordPerfect's search and replace function in two different ways:

1 You can allow WordPerfect to go straight through the document 'searching and replacing' as requested *without* stopping for confirmation from you.

2 You can ask WordPerfect to stop every time it has found the 'search' word and *wait for your confirmation* before it 'replaces' the word.

The latter method is safer, particularly in examinations.

To carry out a global search and replace with confirmation

Search
Replace

1 Position the cursor at the top of the document.

2 Press: **Alt + F2**

3 Press: **Y** (at **w/Confirm Y/N?**)

4 Type: **word to search for** (at **→ Srch:**)
(See handy tips on 'case' and common letter combinations.)

5 Press: **F2**

6 Type: **replacement word** (at **Replace with:**)

7 WordPerfect will stop at the first occurrence of the word to be searched and the question **Confirm? Y/N** will be displayed at the bottom left of screen. Key in **Y for Yes** to confirm that the replacement is correct (or **N for No** to leave as it is).

8 Continue until all replacements have been completed. (See handy tip on setting a 'beep' to confirm end of search.)

Handy tip

Upper and lower case in search and replace

If you want to search for a word that contains *upper case* (capital) letters, you must key in the word in *lower case* after the question '**→ Srch:**'.

If you ask WordPerfect to search for text in upper case characters it will find the text but it will not find the same text in lower case. *For example*: Searching for '**Search**' will find 'Search' but will *not* find '**search**'.

However, searching for '**search**' will find both '**search**' *and* '**Search**'.

Handy tip

Setting up the 'beep' option for end of search or failed search

You can ask WordPerfect to 'beep' to let you know when the *search* option has *finished*, or if the search option has *failed*.

Version 5.0:

Press: **Shift + F1** *(Set-up key)*
Press: **5** *(Initial Settings)*
Press: **1** *(Beep Options)*
Press: **3** *(Beep on Search Failure)*
Press: **Y** *(for Yes)*
Press: **F7** *(to exit this menu)*

Version 5.1:

Press: **Shift + F1** *(Set-up key)*
Press: **3** *(Environment)*
Press: **2** *(Beep Options)*
Press: **3** *(Beep on Search Failure)*
Press: **Y** *(for Yes)*
Press: **F7** *(to exit this menu)*

File
Setup
Environment
Beep Options

Handy tip

Common letter combinations in search and replace

When WordPerfect is searching for text it finds exactly what you requested every time it occurs in the document. This can be a disadvantage if you ask WordPerfect to search for a common combination of letters such as 'one' because not only will it stop at 'one' but it could also stop at 'tone', 'money', 'onerous', and many other words within a document.

To avoid this, key in the text you wish to search for with *a space before and after it. For example*, at the prompt '➔ **Srch:**' you would key in **(space)one(space)**.

It is still advisable to use the *w/Confirm* (confirmation) option because the system just described would not find 'one,' in the text because of the comma following the word.

Allocation of clear line spaces in double line spacing

In WordPerfect, it is not possible to leave an *even number of clear line spaces* within a document by inserting hard returns *if that document is formatted to double line spacing*.

Use the following procedure if you are required to do this:

1 Position cursor immediately after last character of line before insertion of clear spaces is required.

2 Change line spacing to **1** (**Shift** + **F8** Format menu)

3 Insert required number of hard returns, e.g. seven returns to leave six clear lines.

4 Re-set line spacing to **2**.

Note: to leave an *odd number of clear line spaces* while in double line spacing format simply press return the required number of times, e.g. to leave seven clear lines, position cursor immediately after last character of line before insertion of clear spaces is required and press return four times.

Checking the space between two blocks of text

You can check that you have left the correct number of clear line spaces simply by placing the cursor in the first clear line space and pressing ↓ to move the cursor down one (or two) lines at a time, counting as you go along.

Flush right

You can align text at the right margin automatically

like this!

Layout
Justify
Right

Press: **Alt** + **F6** (cursor jumps to right margin)

Type: **The text which is to be right-aligned**

Press: ↵

Headers, footers and page numbering on one document

In the RSA Stage II examination you may be asked to insert a header, a footer and page numbering within one document. Make sure that these features are *not* set to appear in the same position on a document as they may be printed superimposed on top of each other.
If you are not given definite instructions on the positioning of these features, use your own judgement.

3.16 **Exercise 3b.**

Follow steps 3.1 to 3.4 to set the format for the document:

Header (flush right):	Shoppers Guide
Footer (bottom left):	LETTERS
Page numbering:	bottom right of every page
Right margin:	ragged or justified
Line spacing:	double line spacing

3.17 Retrieve your file **EX2B** and follow steps 3.6 and 3.7 to delete unwanted text.

3.18 Amend the text in Exercise 3b as shown, making new pages where you think they should be.

LETTERS PAGE — spaced caps and centre and copy to end of document leaving 3 clear lines before it.

I recently received a request from your organisation for a contribution to your Consumer Information column, which I have pleasure in setting out below.

NOT AT ITS BEST? — underline — 'A'

There is no reason why you should not buy overdue products because the shopkeeper is obliged to provide goods which meet a certain quality. ~~they must not be "bad" or "off".~~ Even if you buy such goods at a reduced price, your legal rights are not affected. If you are unable to obtain satisfaction from the shop manager, contact the local Trading Standards Officer ~~through~~ at the Town Hall.

remove indent

Most food producers need to maintain ~~a good~~ their ~~their~~ reputation and they ~~will usually~~ take ~~any~~ complaints very seriously indeed. It is often a good idea to write to the Managing Director of an organisation enclosing, if possible, a sample of the defective goods. You may have your costs refunded and sometimes a free gift or sample is sent to you as a token of goodwill.

~~T S Orwen (correct date inserted for 1st Friday of next month)~~

You may be ~~It is possible that you are already~~ aware of the fact that ~~it is not unknown for~~ certain people ~~to~~ take advantage of a manufacturer's generosity by frequently returning 'faulty' products. However, most manufacturers keep records of these transactions so it is not a practice which I would recommend and it involves ~~more time and~~ a lot of effort and expense ~~than it is worth~~.

Indent ½" at left

My local shop sometimes sells goods at the end of their 'sell by' date at reduced prices. Is it safe to buy these?

move para to 'A'

single-spacing for 'questions' paras please

'B'

~~Although there is considerable expense in postage, some people have almost made a part-time job out of this hobby! Do you think that an extra paragraph to this effect would be useful or relevant for your readers?~~

~~Please let me know your decision both on the submitted text and the additional information.~~

Indent ½" at left

I want to buy good ~~food~~ for my children. Can I believe what the mfrs put on their labels?

The 1984 Food Labelling Regulations allowed the public to see exactly what they were eating although some of the names and numbers did not have much meaning.

leave 4 clear lines

As a result of pressure from certain organizations ~~groups~~, many of the unnecessary ~~unwanted~~ chemicals have been removed from pre-packed ~~foods~~ & mfrs now actively promote the 'wholesome' nature of their goods. However, as consumers we need to be wary of being ~~fooled~~ by claims such as:

inset by 12 spaces & use single spacing

- no added colour
- no additives
- no artificial ingredients
- no preservatives.

~~These~~ Such claims may ~~hold~~ be true for a product but this does not mean that the food is nutritious. Always read the ingredient list.

(FOOD ADDITIVES) — move to 'B'

~~I hope to hear from you as soon as possible on my article on food additives as you said you may be interested in this.~~

~~I enclose my business card so that you may telephone me. I am in full-time employment so you can reach me between the hours of 9.00 am and 5.00 pm at my business number. After 6.00 pm I can be contacted at home.~~

Pure & Simple?

Flavour is a misleading description – a 'raspberry flavour' ~~food~~ need not contain any raspberry at all!

A 'raspberry flavoured' ~~food~~ shd ~~get~~ obtain a large part of its flavour from raspberries, whereas a 'raspberry' food must be made w whole raspberries. Secret ingredients can creep into some goods. Small amounts of preservatives and sugar do not have to be declared so it is difficult to be sure whether products are really 'pure' and 'natural'.

Some of the descriptions on ~~food~~ labels sound vague, eg 'flavour', 'pure', "natural". What do they really mean?

(Display this para like other questions)

(Please search for 'goods' and replace with 'products' throughout document)

(Leave 3 clear lines here)

(Copy heading 'L— P—' here)

3.19 Spellcheck and proofread your document, checking for consistency of presentation.

3.20 View your document as a final check.

3.21 Save and print a copy of your work. Use the filename **EX3B**.

Printing out arrangements in the RSA Stage II Part 1 examination

You are given 12 sheets of A4 paper in this examination. This is usually sufficient paper to be able to print out *one draft* copy of each task during the examination time and *one final* copy.

The printing of the final copies of the tasks in this examination is done outside the examination time of one-and-a-quarter hours *by the invigilator*.

No amendments may be made to the text after that time has expired.

You are allowed to insert special characters, such as accents, on to the final copies after the examination time.

The invigilator at your examination centre will explain the procedures to be followed for printing in that centre.

Printing marked files from the List Files screen

In Unit 1 you were given instructions on printing your work from the list files screen. In WordPerfect it is possible to speed up the printing process when you want to print more than one file. Each file can be 'marked' with an asterisk (*) at the List Files screen, and when the print command is given WordPerfect will print all the marked files.

You may mark *any number* of the files shown on the directory or *all* of the files shown on the directory.

To mark *selected files* on the list files screen

Position cursor on required file

Type: * *(asterisk)*
* will be shown after file name

Repeat the procedure for all files required.

To mark *all files* on the list files screen

Press: **Home**
Type: *
All files will be marked with *

To remove * marking from files on the list files screen

Press: **Home**
Type: *
* will be removed from all files

This unit contains three exercises to be used as revision of the skills you learned in Units 1, 2 and 3. Work through the consolidation tasks one after the other, printing a *draft* copy for checking (from the List Files screen) as you go along.

Print your final copies of the three tasks by marking the three files with an asterisk (*) at the List Files screen as previously described.

Follow the same procedure for Consolidation 2; also if you are using past examination papers for practice.

Exercise Con1a

SYNOPSIS OF PRESENTATION

A wide range of everyday things can be turned into wine and the result are often very palatable and cheap to produce. Berries, flowers, vegetables, fruits, leaves and weeds can all be trans formed into into intresting and colorful drinks.

Many suitable ingrediants can be found in your garden (or in someone else's) so it is not allways necessary to visit the greengrocer. You don't need to spend alot of money on equipment and their are many shops and supermarkets offering everything you willneed. However, you must always take grate care in hygiene just as yo would if you were preparing food.

Available Wenesdays from

Identify the 14 errors in the above passage and key in a correct copy. The date to be inserted is the 2nd Wed of next month. Save as CON1A and print a copy.

Compare final document with handwritten draft.

SYNOPSIS OF PRESENTATION ← (bold)

Please justify R margin and change line length to 52

A wide range of everyday things can be turned into wine and the results are often very palatable and cheap to produce. Berries, flowers, vegetables, fruits, leaves and weeds can all be transformed into interesting and colourful drinks.

Many suitable ingredients can be found in your garden (or in someone else's) so it is not always necessary to visit the greengrocer. You don't need to spend a lot of money on equipment and there are many shops and supermarkets offering everything you will need. However, you must always take great care in hygiene just as you would if you were preparing food.

Available wednesdays from ——

Exercise Con1b

Please key in the letter below, using a ragged right margin. Standardise layout and presentation and retrieve the synopsis (CON1A) where indicated. (Restore line length to 62 on retrieved text). Save as CON1B and print one copy.

FOR THE A ______ OF THE SPEAKER'S SEC

Ref PC/WP/CON1B

Greenbank Centre
Greenbank Lane
DERBY
DE6 7JL

Dr Sirs

WINE-MAKING (bold + underline)

I was pleased to rec yr request for a presentation on the above topic wh I think wd be of interest to members of yr ~~Club~~ ~~org~~. A synopsis is given below.

(Insert text from CON1A here)

I wd be obliged if you cd let me know the date you wd prefer as a p as I have other organizations regularly contacting me, & I need a certain amount of time to make sure that I have a sufficiently wide range of wines to bring along to a demonstration. [A special feature of my talk is the opp to taste the different wines as well as being able to take away a copy of the easiest recipes. I will supply the wine if you wl supply the glasses! I enclose one copy of my Recipes sheet wh you are welcome to photocopy as necy.

Exercise Con1b *continued*

My talk usually lasts for about one hour, followed by approx half an hour for tasting & questions. I could be at yr Centre at 1830 hours. ✓ If the talk ~~began~~ ~~commenced~~ at 7.00pm, I wd anticipate leaving at approx 9pm. I do not charge a fee but wd be obliged if you could ~~give me~~ let me have the token sum of 5 pounds to cover exps.

There are some items of wine making equipment wh I wd like to show you, & I wd need a large table to accommodate these ~~items~~.

Perhaps you could let me have a map and directions if poss to help me to find the G—— centre. It wd also be of great assistance to me if you could let me know where I can park my car when I arrive. There is quite a lot of carrying to be done both before and after the presentation so the nearer I can ~~drive~~ get to the Centre, the better.

I look forward to hearing from you.

Yrs ffly

PENNY CROFTON (MRS)

Exercise Con1c

Retrieve your file CON1B yourinitials and delete the ref, date, name, address, salutation and complimentary close. Save as CON1C and print a copy.
Use the header - WINES FROM YOUR GARDEN - at top centre of every page and number the pages at the bottom right. Keep pages as shown, use either ragged or justified margin and double line-spacing.

(COUNTRY)
WINE-MAKING ← spaced caps and centre

I was pleased to receive your request for a presentation on the above topic which I think would be of interest to members of your organisation. A synopsis is given below.

SYNOPSIS OF PRESENTATION

COPY TO (*)

A wide range of everyday things can be turned into wine and the results are often very palatable and cheap to produce. Berries, flowers, vegetables, fruits, leaves and weeds can all be transformed into interesting and colourful drinks.

(leave 10 clear lines for diagram)

Many suitable ingredients can be found in your garden (or in someone else's) so it is not always necessary to visit the greengrocer. You don't need to spend a lot of money on equipment and there are many shops and supermarkets offering everything you will need. However, you must always take great care in hygiene just as you would if you were preparing food. MOVE TO (**)

Available Wednesdays from (correct date inserted for 2nd Wednesday of next month)

I would be obliged if you could let me know the date you would prefer as soon as possible as I have other organisations regularly contacting me, and I need a certain amount of time to make sure that I have a sufficiently wide range of wines to bring along to a demonstration.

(PAGE 1)

Exercise Con1c *continued*

Basic Facts (PAGE 2)

During my talk you had
~~A special feature of my talk is~~ the opportunity to taste the different wines. ~~as well as being able to take away a copy of the easiest recipes.~~ ~~I will supply the wine if you will supply the glasses!~~ ~~I enclose one copy of~~ My Recipes sheet ~~which you are welcome to photocopy as necessary~~. gives some easy recipes.

~~My talk usually lasts for about one hour, followed by approximately half an hour for tasting and questions. I could be at your Centre is 1830 hours. If the talk began at 1900 hours, I would anticipate leaving at approximately 2100 hours. I do not charge a fee but would be obliged if you could let me have the token sum of 5 to cover expenses.~~

The main stages of wine-making are:

Inset by 8 spaces and use single spacing with a clear line between items

1 Extraction of flavour & colour
2 Addition of other ingredients & fermenting
3 Straining
4 Fermenting
5 Racking
6 Bottling
7 Storing – for at least six months

Yeast is the most important ingredient in wine making – it must be wine yeast – and a yeast nutrient shd be added.

NUTRIENT

The main ingredient is the fruit, vegetables, flowers or herbs wh give the wine its individual colour, smell and taste

single spacing

Sugar must be carefully weighed before it is made into a syrup (ie dissolved in hot water) and added to the 'must'.

Exercise Con1c

continued

← make into a heading (PAGE 3)

~~There are some items of~~ (wine-making equipment) ~~which I would like to show you, and I would need a large table to accommodate these.~~

~~Perhaps you could let me have directions and a map if possible to help me to find the Greenbank Centre. It would also be of great assistance to me if you could let me know where I can park my car when I arrive. There is quite a lot of carrying to be done both before and after the presentation so the nearer I can get to the Centre, the better.~~

~~I look forward to hearing from you.~~

It is not necy to spend a lot of money on special ~~utensils~~ ~~equipment~~. You probably have most things in yr kitchen already. (**) ←MOVE sentence here — single spacing

Many supermarkets have a range of wine-making equipment and there are specialist shops for the ~~keen~~ enthusiast. Perhaps one of the most helpful aids is yr cellar book where you can record details (of each wine)

You can have great fun, if you have artistic leanings, in designing your own labels.

(leave 7 clear lines for label diagram)

Any kind of bottle will do for your wine provided it is a wine bottle. Restaurants are usually happy to give away their empties. You will also need: — single spacing

- corks
- bottle brush
- siphon hose
- corking tool
- straining cloths

single spacing and indent by 1" from left

(Change wine-making to country wine-making except in headings)

(*) ←COPY sentence here & put in double-spacing

To complete a given form on the word processor you can operate a **search** command to locate 'entry points'. Entry points are simply marked points at which relevant information is to be inserted against a heading or item. After searching for an entry point you should delete it and then insert the relevant piece of information in its place.

In the Stage II examination the form will already have been keyed in for you. For the purposes of this book, however, you will have to key in the form(s) yourself.

Search command

WordPerfect can search through your document forwards or backwards, enabling you to locate quickly any string of word(s) or character(s) (or codes) wherever they appear.

Search

Search Forward

Search Backward

Press: **F2** to search *forwards*
(If you want to search *backwards*, press the ↑ arrow key – you can press the ↓ arrow key to send the search forwards again. Pressing **Shift** + **F2** also operates a backwards search.)

Key in character(s) or word(s) to search for. *Do not press the return key or the hard return will be included in the search!*

Press: **F2** again to begin the search

WordPerfect locates the first occurrence of the string searched for and places the cursor immediately to the right of it.

Press: ← **Del** (backspace delete key) to delete unwanted entry

Key in replacement text

Repeat search

Search Next

Press: **F2** again

The same search string appears on screen. WordPerfect always assumes you want the last string searched for until you enter something different.

Press: **F2** to locate the next occurrence

Continue with repeat search until * **Not Found** * appears on screen

Replacing the entry point with information

Look carefully at the content of the text you are presented with. It will be up to you to use your initiative and extract the appropriate information required for insertion on to the form.

Your style of presentation should be consistent, unless it is specified otherwise.

If you are entering information that is to take up more than one line, e.g. an address, you will first need to set a *tab* in place of the 'entry point' so that the lines begin at the same point, for example:

If the form shows: Address: @

Search for and delete the **@**
Set a left-aligned tab at the point where the '@' sign was positioned

Key in the address, using the tab setting to position the start of each address line

The form will now show: Address: 45 Ridings Lane
Suftborough
LEEDS

Typeover mode in form entry

Where there are two entry points on the same line you will have to use typeover mode (the **Ins** key). This will allow you to insert the information at the first entry point on the line without pushing the second one out of place, although it may appear to do so when you first key in the text. However, when you move to the next entry point, the text should 'jump' back into place.

(If the second item has been set and reached by using a tab setting, it 'jumps' back into place – if the spacebar is used, it is pushed out when text is entered.)

4.1 Exercise 4a.

Key in the form below, following the layout exactly as shown.

Delete all existing tabs
Set a left-aligned tab at 40 (for the 'Tel No' entry)
Save your work – use the filename: **FORM4A**

```
                 BRITANNIA BULBS ORDER FORM
                       26 Rocks Road
                         Sheffield
                          S4 7JB

Customer Name: @
Address: @
Post Code: @                          Tel No: @

Bulbs Type: @
Variety: @
Cat No: @
Quantity: @
Price: @
Date of Order: @
Method of Payment: @

-------------------------------------------------------
TO BE COMPLETED BY DESPATCH DEPARTMENT

Despatch Date ........... Despatched by ................
```

4.2 Exercise 4b.

Clear your screen. Key in the form below, following the layout exactly as shown.

Delete all existing tabs
Set a left-aligned tab at 55 (for the 'Branch No' and 'To' entries)
Save your work – use the filename: **FORM4B**

```
W H BRIDGES & CO
SALES PROMOTION - WEEKEND RESIDENTIAL

PERSONNEL ACCOMMODATION DETAILS

Branch: $                                             Branch No: $

Branch Tel No: $

No of Personnel attending: $
Name(s) of Personnel: $

Date of Residential: From: $                          To: $

Accommodation required: $

Attendance confirmed on (date): $
```

4.3 **Exercise 4c.**

Clear your screen. Retrieve the file **FORM4A**. To complete the form use the *search* facility to locate each occurrence of the @ entry point. Delete the @, then extract the relevant information from the letter below and insert in its place.

Save and *print* a copy of your work – use the filename **EX4C**.

Woodnook Cottage
Woodnook Close
BRADFORD BD5 TR2
Tel No: 0274 384572

15 July 1992

Dear Sir/Madam

I would like to place an order with you for 3 dozen Tulips (Queen Alicia variety) priced at £2.35 per dozen. The catalogue number is TU3782. I enclose a cheque to cover cost of Tulips and packaging.

Yours faithfully

J Smithies

J Smithies (Mrs)

4.4 **Exercise 4d.**

Clear your screen. Retrieve the file **FORM4A** again and complete the form, this time using the information given in the telephone message below.

Save and *print* a copy of your work – use the filename **EX4D**.

TELEPHONE MESSAGE

FROM: Walter Riley
4 Bridge Lane
Huddersfield
HD2 8FL Tel No: 0484 37625

TO: Sales Department

MESSAGE

Mr Riley rang to order 5 dozen crocus bulbs, cat no CR2212 @ £1.50 per dozen. He wants the Mixed Variety and has paid in full by VISA

RECEIVED BY: Kate Davies DATE: 16 July 1992

4.5 Exercise 4e.

Clear your screen. Retrieve the file **FORM4B** and complete the form using the information given in the memorandum below.

Save and *print* a copy of your work – use the filename **EX4E**.

M E M O R A N D U M

From: Chris Blanchard, Manager
Ref: LEEDS Branch No 346

To: Head Office

Date: 27 July 1992

RE: WEEKEND RESIDENTIAL - SALES PROMOTION

I am pleased to confirm that 2 members of staff will be able to attend the weekend residential sales promotion. One will be myself and the other is my assistant, Diane Whitely.

We will require overnight accommodation for 2nd and 3rd of August 1992 - 2 single rooms with bath please.

Can you ring me at the Branch Tel No (0532 683462) asap with travel details.

Using standard paragraphs

Many letters have some parts in them that are identical in content. This can mean keying in the same portions of text over and over again, e.g. company addresses, standard paragraphs or the 'Yours sincerely' closure at the end.

With WordPerfect you can store these standard paragraphs as separate files and then retrieve them into any document as and when required.

To set up standard paragraphs

1. Key in the text for each paragraph (or portion of text)
2. Save each paragraph (or portion of text) as a separate file in the usual way. If you use easily identifiable filenames it will help you to retrieve the correct file, e.g. **SINCE** for a 'Yours sincerely' closure, or **FAITH** for a 'Yours faithfully' closure.

To retrieve the standard paragraph file into your document

Method 1

```
File
Retrieve
```

Position cursor at place you want the text to be inserted
Press: **Shift + F10**
Document to be retrieved appears at bottom left of screen
Key in the filename and press **return**

Method 2

```
File
List Files
```

Position cursor at place you want the text to be inserted
Press: **F5** ↵ (to bring up list files)
Position cursor on filename
Press: **1** (Retrieve)
Answer: **Retrieve into current document Y/N?: Y**(es)

After using either method to retrieve the file, press **PgDn** to position the cursor at the end of the document to save time scrolling down.

Your standard letter needs to be well displayed. In the Stage II examination you must standardize on layout, line spacing and heading styles. You will also need to emphasize text (bold, underline, etc), and extract information from another task.

Don't forget to insert the date in the correct position!

5.1 **Exercise 5a.**

Clear your screen. Key in the following standard paragraphs and save each one using the filenames indicated.

Filename	
ADDRESS	BRITANNIA BULBS 26 Rocks Road Sheffield S4 7JB Tel No: 0742 472831
ORDER	Thank you for your recent order for a selection of our bulbs.
ENQUIRY	Thank you for your recent enquiry regarding a selection of our bulbs.
INSTOCK	We are pleased to advise you that these items are in stock and should arrive within the next fourteen days.
OUTSTOCK	We are sorry to advise you that these items are currently out of stock.
PRICE	Please find enclosed an up-to-date price list and this season's brochure.
SINCE	Yours sincerely BRITTANIA BULBS Sales Department
FAITH	Yours faithfully BRITTANIA BULBS Sales Department

5.2 **Exercise 5b.**

Clear your screen. Key in the letter below with a ragged right margin. Retrieve the relevant standard paragraphs (using the filenames given,
e.g. **ADDRESS**) and insert at the points marked.

Save and *print* a copy of your work – use the filename **EX5B**.

(ADDRESS)

(today's date)

Mrs J Smithies
Woodnook Cottage
Woodnook Close
BRADFORD BD5 2TR

Dr. Mrs Smithies

Re your order of 15 July 1992 ← (please emphasise this heading)

(ORDER)

Our records show yr. order was for: 3 dozen Tulips, Queen Alicia variety at a cost of (refer to Exercise 4.3 for this information) per dozen.

(INSTOCK)

A rec. for your ~~cheque~~ Visa will be enclosed w. the bulbs, along with instructions for planting. [We look forward to hearing from/you again.

(SINCE)

(Follow the line spacing of the paragraph beginning "Our records show ......")

5.3 **Exercise 5c.**

Clear your screen. Key in the letter below with a justified right margin. Retrieve the relevant standard paragraphs (using the filenames given) and insert at the points marked.

When following the instruction marked with an * remember to alter the right margin setting in order to allocate the required space.

Save and *print* a copy of your work – use the filename **EX5C**.

ADDRESS

please emphasise the words underlined with a ~~~~

(today's date)

Mr Walter Riley
4 Bridge Lane
HUDDERSFIELD
HD2 FL8

all text to start from left margin as in the paragraph which begins "Our records ...."

Dear Mr Riley

ORDER

Our records show that your order was for 5 Mixed dozen Crocus bulbs, Cat No CR2212, and that you have already paid in full by (refer to Exercise 4.4 for payment type).

OUTSTOCK In fact, your order was taken from a cat. which was out-of-date. PRICE

alternative

We will be pleased to supply you with an ~~optional~~ selection from the new cat. or offer you a full refund.

* leave a space here 2" across by 1" down for a voucher

Please accept our apologies for any incon. caused, along with the attached 50p voucher.

SINCE

Encs

5.4 **Exercise 5d.**

Clear your screen. Key in the letter below with a ragged right margin. Retrieve the relevant standard paragraphs and insert at the points marked.

Save and *print* a copy of your work – use the filename **EX5D**.

(ADDRESS)

(today's date)

H Jones & Son
Beaver Works
Drye Rd.
HALIFAX
HX4 8UY

(make all paragraphs the same style as the first one)

Dr. Sirs

(ENQUIRY)

We are pleased to hear of your ~~intentions~~ plans to improve the firm's car-parking area with shrubbery and bulbs, and ~~and~~ wd. like to take this opp. to tell you about our new Garden Helpline Service. (stet)

Details of this are explained in the accompanying leaflet, along with our ~~burl~~ new Gardener's Helpline Telephone Number. // When re turning your order form, could you please let us know where you saw our advert. as this will assist our marketing dept.

(PRICE)

(FAITH)

Encs

(please use any word processing method to give prominence to the words underlined with ~~~)

In the RSA Stage II examination, the table contains a number of additional features to the tabulation work you completed at Stage I.

In addition to normal editing and tabulation procedures you will also be required to:

- include a footnote
- rearrange the table items in a specified order

Since the table is usually quite large, you will also need to give consideration to making it fit on the page/paper size being used. If you think the table won't quite fit using your normal settings, there are several options open to you:

- reduce the left and right margin settings to half an inch – this is the least amount acceptable
- wrap the text around on to the next line in the column
- reduce the size of the pitch – see section on changing the pitch size

Setting new tabs

Layout
Line

Press: **Shift** + **F8**
Select: **1** (Line) **8** (Tab Set)
Type: **0 ↵** (to get to position 0 on ruler)
Press: **Ctrl** + **End** key (to delete all current tabs)

Enter **L**, **R**, **C**, **D**, along the ruler wherever you want to set a *left*, *right*, *centred* or *decimal* tab setting.

Leader dot tabs

Reposition the cursor on the tab setting already made and press the full stop over it, e.g. **L**(eft) + **.** (full stop) will give you a left-aligned tab setting with a row of leader dots preceding it.

Example: **Mary Smith** .... **Personnel** **Ext 2467**

Press: **F7** (to *exit* the tab menu)
(pressing any other key will not *save* the changes!)
Press: **F7** (to return your document)

Footnotes

A footnote is a piece of information placed at the end of each page (or document) which explains, in more depth, a particular point made within the body of the text.

A footnote symbol, such as *, is placed in the body of the text next to the point which needs further explanation. The same symbol is repeated at the end of the page or document with the explanatory text next to it. If more than one footnote is needed you can use two asterisks – **.

There is *no space before* the footnote symbol in the body of the text.

There is at least *one space between* the footnote symbol and the explanatory text at the end of the page/document.

This is a simple, manual method of footnote entry. (WordPerfect has a much more sophisticated facility of entering footnotes but the authors feel this is not necessarily appropriate for students at intermediate level. However, you may consult your user manual or your tutor if you wish.)

Changing pitch size

If you have a lot of information to fit on the page you may need to change the size of the pitch. Word processors usually use 10-pitch (10CPI – characters per inch) by default. WordPerfect has a facility that will allow you to select a smaller pitch size such as 12-pitch (12 CPI) – this will enable you to fit more data on to the table.

Your table should either be all in 10-pitch or all in 12-pitch – not a mixture!

```
Font
Base Font
```

Press: **Ctrl + F8**
Select: **4** (Base Font)
(The pitch in current use is asterisked on the list displayed.)
Highlight your selection, e.g. **12 CPI**
Press: **1** (Select)

Any changes made through the **Ctrl + F8** Base Font menu will only affect the document you are working on – they will not permanently alter the default settings.

Important: the type of printer you are using will determine which fonts can be supported, as some printers are not capable of utilising all of WordPerfect's features. Check with your tutor or printer manual and/or print a draft test copy to try out the different effects.

Working out tab setting positions for table

1 Decide whether or not you need to alter the pitch size or reduce the margin settings to half-an-inch. If necessary, make any changes to pitch or margins *before* setting the tabs. You need to take into account the following:

- There is often one column that is variable in width – it can be made narrower if the text is narrative in style (i.e. text 'runs on', and is not made up of separate items) by putting the text on to more than one line. This means it may not be necessary to change the pitch size or the margins.

The following options are available:

- You could keep left and right margins at 1 in and use 10-pitch.
- If the table will not fit on the default settings, you could reduce the left and right margins to $\frac{1}{2}$ in and keep 10-pitch.
- If the table still will not fit, you could set the left and right margins to 1 in and change to 12-pitch.

When calculating the amount of 'character space' across an A4 page, note that:

- If you are using 10-pitch CPI with left and right margin settings of 1 in your right margin will be at 72 and you will have 62 character spaces across the page.
- If you are using 10-pitch CPI with left and right margin settings of $\frac{1}{2}$ in your right margin will be at 77 and you will have 72 character spaces across the page.
- If you are using 12-pitch CPI with left and right margin settings of 1 in your right margin will be at 87 and you will have 76 character spaces across the page.

2 At this point, you could bring up the *ruler line* on screen to check your margin and tab stops:

Edit
Window

Press: **Ctrl** + **F3**
Select: **1** (Window)
Key in: **23** ↵ (against Number of Lines in this window: 24)

(You may remove the ruler when you no longer require it by repeating the above procedure, keying in 24 lines for the window instead of 23.)

3 Enter the tab menu (**Shift** + **F8**, **1**, **8**) and delete all existing tab settings.

4 Set tabs for the table. The type of data in the table will determine whether you should:

- work backwards from the right margin to set the tabs,
- work forwards from the left margin to set the tabs, or
- use a combination of these two methods if the variable width column is not at extreme left or right of the table.

As a general rule, where you have a 'variable column' (i.e. a column containing text and leader dots, or with 'narrative' text which can sensibly run on to more than one line) it is easier to set tabs to mark the columns of 'fixed' width first.

You should work forwards from the left margin (Method 1) until you reach the variable column. You should then work backwards from the right margin (Method 2) until you reach the variable column from the other direction. The space that is left after you have done this is automatically allocated to the variable column (there is no need to calculate a specific number of characters).

If the table does not contain leader dots, and all the column entries are meant to fit on to one line, you should space forwards from the left margin (Method 1).

Method 1

Position cursor at the left margin on ruler line in the tab set menu. Press the right arrow key once for every character in the longest line of the first column, plus an extra three times for the space between the first and second columns. (Don't forget to check the column heading – it may be longer than the items in the column itself.) Set a **L**(eft-aligned) tab.

Repeat the procedure for the number of characters in the longest line of the second column plus three for the space, and set a second tab. Continue in this way for all the column tab settings in the table.

Method 2

Position cursor at the right margin on ruler line in the tab set menu. Press the left arrow key once for every character in the longest line of the last column. (Don't forget to check the column heading – it may be longer than the items in the column itself.) Set a **L**(eft-aligned) tab.

Move to the left three times for the space between the columns, then press the left arrow key once for every character in the longest line of the next-to-last column and set a **L**(eft-aligned) tab.

5 Use **F7** to exit the tab menu, and return to your document. Check that the correct number of tabs is shown on the ruler line, then remove the ruler line if you wish.

6 Use the tab key to move between the columns and enter the appropriate information into each column.

WordPerfect version 5.1 – table facility

The table facility of version 5.1 offers an alternative method of setting up a table, and many of the Stage II table tasks could be completed using this feature.

Instructions for using the table command have not been included in this book, as the authors feel that this feature may not be easily attainable by students at the intermediate level. However, you may consult your user manual or your tutor if you wish.

6.1 **Exercise 6a.**

Clear your screen. You are going to enter the table below for Britannia Bulbs. It will fit on an A4 page in 10-pitch.

1 Delete the existing tab settings. Then enter **L**(eft) tab settings for the column headings at: **48**, **57**, **65**

2 Key in main headings and column headings of the table: **BRITTANIA BULBS** to **SPRING FLOWERING** inclusive.

3 You now need to change:

- the **CAT NO** tab setting to a *leader dot* tab (so the entries will be preceded by a row of leader dots)
- the **PRICE** tab setting to a *decimal* tab (so the figures in the price column will wrap around the decimal point)

Go back into the tab menu. Position the cursor at **48** – *do not* delete the setting, but simply key in a full stop over the top – you have now told WordPerfect to put leader dots to the left of this tab setting.

Delete the **L**(eft) tab setting at **57**. Set a **D**(ecimal) tab stop at **59**. Exit the tab menu.

4 Key in the first entry for column 1: **CROCUS** – **Purple Delight**. Press the space bar once, then press the tab key to move to the second column. (A row of leader dots appears between the columns; although on screen the last dot appears to go right up to the next character, when you print out there will be a space left between. Use the View Document option from the print menu to view this on screen.)

5 Key in the entry for column 2: **CR2213**. Press the tab key to move to the third column. Key in the price: **1.65** – note how the figures automatically wrap around the decimal tab. Press the tab key and enter the data for the final **UNIT** column: **dozen**

6 Repeat the above procedure for each row.

7 *Save* your work – use the filename **EX6A**. Don't print out at this stage.

BRITTANIA BULBS

LATEST ADDITIONS TO THE CATALOGUE:

BULB DESCRIPTION	CAT NO	PRICE	UNIT
SPRING FLOWERING			
CROCUS - Purple Delight	CR2213	£1.65	dozen
TULIP - Princess Orange Maiden . . .	TU3784	£3.50	dozen
IRIS - Lilac Lady	IRI21	£2.40	dozen
ANENOME - Rainbow Palette	AN8167	£4.55	fifty
SPECIAL SPRING MIXTURE*	SB14	£10.00	hundred
AUTUMN FLOWERING			
GLADIOLUS - White Heat	GL36	£0.75	three
ZEPHYRANTHES - Autumn Breeze	ZE13	£0.45	each
ACIDANTHERA - Princess Rhia	AC3334	£0.95	each
SPECIAL AUTUMN MIXTURE	SB14	£15.00	hundred

* Also available in Units of 500 at a Discount Price of £35.00

Rearranging items in table

In the RSA Stage II examination you will be asked to rearrange or sort the table into a particular order. There are several ways to do this. The choice is yours.

Method 1

Before you begin to key in the table use a piece of scrap paper to note down, in advance, the order in which the entries should be keyed in.

Method 2

Key in the entries as they are displayed, then use *block* and *move* functions to rearrange the items in the required order.

Method 3

Key in the entries as they are displayed, then use WordPerfect's *line sort* facility to sort them into the required order. To use line sort, the data must be set out in rows and columns. You can choose to sort alphabetically (A–Z), or numerically (0,1,2,3,4...). Line sort is only effective if all entries on the table take up one line only, otherwise secondary lines will be included in the sort.

Line sort

Although you can sort a whole file, you will usually only want to sort part of your document. This should be blocked first with **F12** or **Alt** + **F4** keys.

First, *Block* the portion of text you wish to sort:

Tools
Sort

Press: **Ctrl** + **F9**
(Your screen should now be split in half to show the Line Screen)
Select: **3** (Keys) to specify column number to sort on
(The cursor moves to the *Typ* heading which determines whether the sort is to be alphanumeric (a) or numeric (n))
Press: ↵ to accept **a**(lphanumeric)
or key in: **n** to specify a numeric sort
(The cursor moves to the *Field* heading where you specify the field number of your first sort key)
Press: ↵ to accept the default of 1, or specify other
(The cursor moves to the *Word* heading where you specify which word to sort by, i.e. if the field contains more than one word, you can choose to sort by word one, two, three etc)
Press: ↵ to accept the default of 1, or specify other
Press: **F7** to exit the definition area
Press: **1** (Perform Action)

To sort in descending order

Repeat the above procedure, but before pressing **1 Perform Action**:

Select: **6** (Order) **2** (Descending)

6.2 **Exercise 6b.**

Retrieve the file **EX6A** if it is not already on your screen. You are now going to rearrange the items in alphabetical order of *bulb description*. However, you must keep the *spring flowering* and *autumn flowering* sections separate.

As you have already entered the data for this exercise, you could not predetermine the order while keying in. As you already know how to use *block* and *move* methods, this would be a good time to try out the *line sort* facility!

6.3 Using **Alt** + **F4** or **F12** keys,

Edit Block

block the five items in the *spring flowering* section – i.e. from the **C** of *CROCUS – Purple Delight* to the last **d** of hundred at the end of the *SPECIAL SPRING MIXTURE* row.

6.4

Tools Sort

Press: **Ctrl** + **F9**
Select: **3** (Keys)
Press: ↵ to accept a(lphanumeric)
Press: ↵ to accept the field default of 1
Press: ↵ to accept the word default of 1
Press: **F7** to exit the definition area
Press: **1** (Perform Action)

The items should now be rearranged into alphabetical order.

6.5 Repeat the sort procedure for the autumn flowering items.

6.6 Let's try sorting the table into numeric order of *price*.

Tools Sort

Block the *spring flowering* items.
Press: **Ctrl** + **F9**
Select: **3** (Keys)
Press: **n** to specify a n(umeric) sort
Press: **3** ↵ to specify the price field (i.e. third column or field)
Press: ↵ to accept the word default of 1
Press: **F7** to exit the definition area
Press: **1** (Perform Action)

The *spring flowering* items should now be rearranged into ascending price order.

6.7 Repeat the numeric sort by price for the autumn flowering items.

6.8 *Save* and *print* a copy of your work – use the filename **EX6B**.

Remember: you can always work out the order of keying in beforehand, or use the *block* and *move* methods if you run into difficulties with *line sort*. As you have just seen, however, line sort is a quick and useful way of sorting data which has been arranged in a 'spreadsheet-type' format.

6.9 Exercise 6c.

Clear your screen. Key in the table below. You can key it in using 10-pitch and reduce the left and right margin settings to half an inch (your right margin will then be at 77). (You do not need to use leader dots.)

Please emphasize the words marked by a X

Save and *print* a copy of your work – use the filename **EX6C**.

W H BRIDGES & CO SALES PROMOTION (centre)

WEEKEND RESIDENTIAL

The personnel following are to be directly involved with the company's new sales promotion scheme. Their names need to be added to the attendance list for the weekend residentials to be held in ~~July~~ August.

BRANCH NO	BRANCH NAME	PAYROLL NO	NAME	DATE OF W/R*
346	LEEDS	24671	DIANE WHITELY	3/8/92
346	LEEDS	23672	CHRIS BLANCHARD	3/8/92
311	BRADFORD	37268	ASHRAF AKBAR	10/8/92
314	SHEFFIELD	37283	MAVIS RAWSON	10/8/92
311	BRADFORD	28473	MARGARET SUNCLIFFE	10/8/92
237	YORK	27346	SUSANNAH BLAKELY	17/8/92
~~237~~	~~YORK~~	~~22366~~	~~IRENE STEAD~~	~~17/8/92~~
237	YORK	18384	CHRISTOPHER BLAND	17/8/92
119	HUDDERSFIELD	36272	STEPHAN ITRYCH	24/9/92
119	HUDDERSFIELD	27474	MARTIN HOLROYD	24/8/92

* The Weekend Residentials start on the dates listed in the above table but a number of personnel will require an overnight stay the previous night – details of these to follow shortly.

(retain date entries in the format shown)

(please re-arrange the table in alphabetical order of surname)

6.10 **Exercise 6d.**

Clear your screen. Key in the table below. Alter the pitch to 12-pitch to make the table fit on an A4 page with the shorter end at the top – you may keep left and right margins set at 1 in.

Please emphasize the words marked by a ~~~~

Don't forget to use a **D**(ecimal) tab for the last column.

Save and *print* a copy of your work – use the filename **EX6D**.

* MUSIC PROMOTIONS LTD

SPECIAL OFFERS

We are pleased to announce this month's special offers. All units are supplied in ~~ash~~ black effect finish. Special discounts are available on bulk orders (twenty-five or more).

leave a space here at least 2" across and ½" down (51mm × 13mm) for a stamp

ITEM DESCRIPTION	SIZE	CAT NO	PRICE
REGENT 3-drawer ~~compact disc~~ audio cassette storage cabinet	14x12x7 in	ZX235	14.99
DEXCEL 2-drawer compact disc storage unit	13x5x16 in	WR114	5.25
~~KORA 3-drawer record storage case~~	~~16x16x14 in~~	~~WT223~~	~~7.99~~
STAVER 4-drawer compact disc library cabinet	12x12x7 in	WR256	12.99
XENON de-luxe audio cassette storage case*	7x7x11 in	ZX551	5.49
NEWSTYLE cassette carousel	7x7x10 in	ZX727	3.99

* This item also available in luxury, green leather-look vinyl.

please re-arrange the table in alphabetical order of ITEM DESCRIPTION

Printing out arrangements in the RSA Stage II Part 2 examination

You are given six sheets of A4 paper – sufficient to be able to print out one draft copy of each task during the examination time, and one final copy for the examiner.

The printing of the final copies of the tasks in this examination is done outside the examination time of one-and-a-quarter hours *by the candidate*.

No amendments may be made to the text after that time has expired and, in WordPerfect, the printing is done from the List Files screen. (*There is no need to retrieve the document to print.*)

You are allowed to insert special characters, such as accents, on to the final copies after the examination time.

The invigilator at your examination centre will explain the procedures to be followed for printing in that centre.

Form completion

Exercise Con2a

Key in the following form exactly as shown below. Save under filename **CON2A**, then clear your screen.

```
THE THREE EAGLES HOTEL

WEDDING RECEPTION BOOKING FORM

NAME $
ADDRESS $
TEL NO $

NO OF GUESTS        ROOM REQUIRED
$                   $

RECEPTION DATE      RECEPTION TIME
$                   $


TYPE OF CATERING REQUIRED
$

COST OF ROOM        COST OF CATERING (per head)
$                   $

DEPOSIT PAID        DATE
$                   $
```

Exercise Con2b

Retrieve the file **CON2A** and complete the form with the appropriate information from the message below.

Save and *print* a copy of your file – use the filename **CON2B**.

<u>Message for Hotel Manager</u>
Susan Bailey of 2 Grandesmere Place, Manchester, called into Reception and left a £50 deposit for the Atlantic Room. She wants to book the room for 150 guests for her wedding reception on Sep 12 between 1.30pm + 4.30pm. We have made a provisional booking for the room at a charge of £55 and £7.50 per head for the CARVERY catering. Can you ring Susan on 061-4782001 to confirm the booking ASAP.

Mary Saville (Receptionist)
18 July

Standard letter

Exercise Con2c

Key in the following standard paragraphs. Save each one under the filename shown.

Filename	
EAGLES	THE THREE EAGLES HOTEL 4 Grandways Road MANCHESTER MN4 ET2
CONFIRM	I am pleased to confirm the provisional booking for your
MENU	Please find enclosed some sample menus of all our catering options.
MAP	I hope the attached map of the Three Eagles location will be of help to any guests travelling to your reception from other areas.
BEST	Best wishes Jane Lumb (MANAGERESS)

Exercise Con2d

Key in the letter below with a justified right margin. Recall the relevant paragraphs and insert at the points marked. *Save* and *print* a copy of your work – use the filename **CON2D**.

EAGLES

(today's date)

use the same style for all the headings, following the style of the last one, ACCOMMODATION

Miss Susan Bailey
2 Grandsmere Place
MANCHESTER

Dear Susan

WEDDING RECEPTION

CONFIRM wedding reception to take place on (refer to Con 2b for the date to insert here)

CATERING

I bel. you have requested CARVERY-style catering @£7.50 per head. As an alternative, you may wish to consider our cold and hot Buffet menus. MENU

Room

You have been allocated the ATLANTIC ROOM which will comfortably hold between 125-160 guests and will therefore accommodate your present guest list.

A fixed charge of £5 ~~#5~~ is payable for the room. Shd. you find you need to cater for additional guests, we can offer a larger room at no extra cost providing you notify us within the next month.

ACCOMMODATION

I understand you have relatives attending the function who wish to book an overnight stay at the Hotel. Please send us details of any requirements as soon as possible.

I shall contact you again in due course to make final arrangements.

BEST

please emphasise all the headings

Encs

Exercise Con2e

Key in the table below. You may alter the line length or pitch if necessary to make it fit on an A4 page with the shorter end at the top. *Save* and *print* a copy of your work – use the filename **CON2E**.

THE THREE EAGLES
4 Grandways Road
MANCHESTER MN4 ET2 } centre

FUNCTION BOOKINGS – SEPTEMBER ← emphasise this heading

Hotel rooms (temporary) ~~have been~~ booked for the following (dates in September. Please arrange for ↷staff to be contracted for all events, but particularly where there are ~~a~~ ~~lot of guests~~ / high guest numbers

leave a space at least 2" across by 1" down (51mm × 25mm) for hotel logo

CLIENT NAME	MENU	COST PER HEAD	GUEST NOS	DATE BOOKED
Betty Walsden	CARVERY	£7.50	100 ⇅	26 SEP
Sebastian MacIntosh	COLD BUFFET	£5.50	145 ⇅	22 SEP
Susan Bailey	CARVERY	£7.50	155	12 SEP
~~Denise Watson~~	~~CARVERY~~	~~£7.50~~	~~145~~	~~12 SEP~~
Anabella Ferrybridge	HOT BUFFET	£6.50	60	13 SEP
David Ridgeway	COLD BUFFET	£5.50	85	20 SEP
Margaret Helm	CARVERY	£7.50	~~110~~ 100	2 SEP
Mohammed Zafar	HOT BUFFET	£6.50	125	8 SEP
Henry Swan	CHEESE/WINE	£4.75*	50	18 SEP

* Cost per head conditional on ~~numbers attending and~~ available house / wines.

operator: retain the abbreviations for the months

please re-arrange the table in order of DATE BOOKED starting with the beginning of the month

Unit 1

Exercise 1a

CALDERGHYLL (REF CMB424)

This mid-terraced house is near the centre of the town and convenient for all amenities. Luxuriously furnished with antiques and equipped with every labour-saving device, this house offers the ideal place for a relaxing break. Accommodation is for 4 people in 2 twin-bedded rooms on the first floor. The ground floor comprises lounge, kitchen and dining room. The first floor bathroom has both bath and shower.

The owner does not object to 1 small dog kept under proper control.

PRICE BAND 12   NB Available from (correct date inserted for 1st Saturday of next month).

Exercise 1b

There is no reason why you should not buy overdue products because the shopkeeper is obliged to provide goods which meet a certain quality - they must not be "bad" or "off". Even if you buy such goods at a reduced price, your legal rights are not affected. If you are unable to obtain satisfaction from the shop manager, contact the local Trading Standards Officer through the Town Hall.

Most food producers need to maintain a good reputation and they will usually take any complaint very seriously indeed. It is often a good idea to write to the Managing Director of an organisation enclosing, if possible, a sample of the defective goods. You may have your costs refunded and sometimes a free gift or sample is sent to you as a token of goodwill.

T S Orwen (correct date inserted for 1st Friday of next month)

Unit 2

Exercise 2a

Name Exercise 2A

Ref EWP/2A

Date of typing

URGENT

Mrs B S Kelly
236 Main Street
Weston
BARNSLEY
BY10 8JJ

Dear Mrs Kelly

CUMBRIAN COTTAGES

Thank you for your letter of (correct date inserted for last Monday) requesting information on self-catering cottages in Cumbria. I have pleasure in setting out below details of the accommodation at "Calderghyll" which is available for the dates which you mentioned.

A booking form is enclosed for your use and I hope that you will find that you are satisfied with "Calderghyll" from the details shown. At this time of year many people are making holiday arrangements and I would suggest that you telephone our bookings section on 061-763205 as soon as possible in order to make a provisional reservation. You can telephone at any time between 8.00 am and 7.00 pm from Monday to Friday and between 10.00 am and 5.00 pm from Saturday to Sunday.

CALDERGHYLL (REF CMB424)

This mid-terraced house is near the centre of the town and convenient for all amenities. Luxuriously furnished with antiques and equipped with every labour-saving device, this house offers the ideal place for a relaxing break. Accommodation is for 4 people in 2 twin-bedded rooms on the first floor. The ground floor comprises lounge, kitchen and dining room. The first floor bathroom has both bath and shower.

The owner does not object to 1 small dog kept under proper control.

PRICE BAND 12 NB Available from (correct date inserted for 1st Saturday of next month).

Exercise 2a

Name Exercise 2A

I would like to take this opportunity of assuring you of the high standards of service which you can expect from our organisation.

We pride ourselves on the careful and thorough processing of enquiries and bookings. All of our properties are regularly inspected and members of staff are available at any time to solve any problems which may arise.

We recommend that you take advantage of our inexpensive insurance cover. The cost is competitive at £4.50 per person per week, and £15.00 for a family (4 to 6 persons).

Please contact me if you would like any further information or advice. I look forward to hearing from you in the near future.

Yours sincerely
RURAL IDYLLS PLC

Elisabeth W Pendragon

Enc

2

Exercise 2b

Name Exercise 2B

Ref TSO/WP/B2

(Date of typing)

FOR THE ATTENTION OF MS W GOOD

The Consumer Guide
172-175 Byre Street
YORK
YO2 1JM

Dear Sirs

LETTERS PAGE

I recently received a request from your organisation for a contribution to your Consumer Information column, which I have pleasure in setting out below.

> **NOT AT ITS BEST?**
>
> There is no reason why you should not buy overdue products because the shopkeeper is obliged to provide goods which meet a certain quality - they must not be "bad" or "off". Even if you buy such goods at a reduced price, your legal rights are not affected. If you are unable to obtain satisfaction from the shop manager, contact the local Trading Standards Officer through the Town Hall.
>
> Most food producers need to maintain a good reputation and they will usually take any complaint very seriously indeed. It is often a good idea to write to the Managing Director of an organisation enclosing, if possible, a sample of the defective goods. You may have your costs refunded and sometimes a free gift or sample is sent to you as a token of goodwill.
>
> **T S Orwen (correct date inserted for 1st Friday of next month)**

It is possible that you are already aware of the fact that it is not unknown for certain people to take advantage of a manufacturer's generosity by frequently returning 'faulty' products. Most manufacturers keep records of these transactions so it is not a practice which I would recommend and it involves more time and effort than it is worth.

Although there is considerable expense in postage, some people have almost made a part time job out of this hobby! Do you think that an extra paragraph to this effect would be useful or relevant for your readers?

Please let me know your decision both on the submitted text and the additional information.

Exercise 2b

Name   Exercise 2B

FOOD ADDITIVES

I hope to hear from you as soon as possible on my article on food additives as you said you may be interested in this.

I enclose my business card so that you may telephone me. I am in full time employment so you can reach me between the hours of 9.00 am and 5.00 pm at my business number. After 6.00 pm I can be contacted at home.

Yours faithfully

T S Orwen (Mr)

Enc

Unit 3

Exercise 3a

Name Exercise 3A

RURAL IDYLLS

C U M B R I A N   C O T T A G E S

Self-catering cottages in Cumbria

At this time of year many people are making holiday arrangements. Telephone our reservations section on 061-763205 as soon as possible in order to make a provisional reservation.

You can telephone at any time between 0800 hrs and 1900 hrs from Monday to Friday and between 0900 hrs and 1700 hrs from Saturday to Sunday.

You can be assured of high standards of service from our organisation. We pride ourselves on the thorough and careful processing of enquiries and reservations. All of our properties are regularly inspected and members of staff are available at any time to solve any problems which may arise.

We recommend that you take advantage of our inexpensive insurance cover. The cost is competitive at £4.50 per person per week, and £15.00 for a family (4 - 6 persons).

THE CALDERBROOK AREA HAS 2 HOUSES WHICH ARE AVAILABLE WITHIN THE DATES REQUIRED.

1

Exercise 3a

Name   Exercise 3A

RURAL IDYLLS

<u>Calderghyll (Ref CMB424)</u>

This mid-terraced house is near the centre of Calderbrook and convenient for all amenities. Luxuriously furnished with antiques and equipped with every labour-saving device, this house offers the ideal place for a relaxing break.

Accommodation is for 4 people in 2 twin-bedded rooms on the first floor. The ground floor comprises lounge, kitchen and dining room. The first floor bathroom has both bath and shower.

The owner does not object to 1 small dog kept under proper control.

PRICE BAND 12   NB Available from (correct date inserted for 1st Saturday of next month).

2

Exercise 3a

Name Exercise 3A

RURAL IDYLLS

Brockholes Cottage (Ref CMB546)

This attractive stone cottage has been renovated to a very high standard. It is particularly well-equipped, having an automatic washer, tumble drier, dishwasher and microwave oven.

Accommodation is for 3 or 4 persons in 2 bedrooms (1 twin, 1 double). There is a comfortable sitting room with a log fire and a separate kitchen/diner. The modern bathroom has a 3-piece suite and there is a separate shower room on the ground floor.

The property has the advantages of:

oil-fired central heating
electricity for cooking
garage for 1 car
private walled garden

The owner does not object to 1 small dog kept under proper control.

The cottage is 1 mile from shops and pub, and many clients have already made reservations.

PRICE BAND 10 NB Available from (correct date inserted for 2nd Saturday of next month).

Exercise 3b

Shoppers Guide

L E T T E R S   P A G E

NOT AT ITS BEST?

My local shop sometimes sells products at the end of their 'sell by' date at reduced prices. Is it safe to buy these?

There is no reason why you should not buy overdue products because the shopkeeper is obliged to provide products which meet a certain quality. Even if you buy such products at a reduced price, your legal rights are not affected. If you are unable to obtain satisfaction from the shop manager, contact the local Trading Standards Officer at the Town Hall.

Most food producers need to maintain their reputation and they take complaints very seriously indeed. It is often a good idea to write to the Managing Director of an organisation enclosing, if possible, a sample of the defective products. You may have your costs refunded and sometimes a free sample or gift is sent to you as a token of goodwill.

LETTERS 1

Exercise 3b

Shoppers Guide

You may be aware of the fact that certain people take advantage of a manufacturer's generosity by frequently returning 'faulty' products. However, most manufacturers keep records of these transactions so it is not a practice which I would recommend and it involves a lot of effort and expense.

FOOD ADDITIVES

> I want to buy good food for my children. Can I believe what the manufacturers put on their labels?

The 1984 Food Labelling Regulations allowed the public to see exactly what they were eating although some of the names and numbers did not have much meaning.

As a result of pressure from certain organisations, many of the unnecessary chemicals have been removed from pre-packed foods and manufacturers now actively promote the 'wholesome' nature of their products.

LETTERS 2

Exercise 3b

Shoppers Guide

However, as consumers we need to be wary of being fooled by claims such as:

no added colour
no additives
no artificial ingredients
no preservatives

Such claims may be true for a product but this does not mean that the food is nutritious. Always read the ingredient list.

PURE AND SIMPLE?

> Some of the descriptions on food labels sound vague, eg 'flavour', 'pure', 'natural'. What do they really mean?

Flavour is a misleading description - a 'raspberry flavour' food need not contain any raspberry at all! A 'raspberry flavoured' food should obtain a large part of its flavour from raspberries, whereas a 'raspberry' food must be made with whole raspberries. Secret ingredients can creep into some products. Small amounts of sugar and preservatives do not have to be declared so it is difficult to be sure whether products are really 'pure' and 'natural'.

L E T T E R S   P A G E

LETTERS 3

Consolidation 1

Exercise Con1a

SYNOPSIS OF PRESENTATION

A wide range of everyday things can be turned into wine and the results are often very palatable and cheap to produce. Berries, flowers, vegetables, fruits, leaves and weeds can all be transformed into interesting and colourful drinks.

Many suitable ingredients can be found in your garden (or in someone else's) so it is not always necessary to visit the greengrocer. You don't need to spend a lot of money on equipment and there are many shops and supermarkets offering everything you will need. However, you must always take great care in hygiene just as you would if you were preparing food.

Available Wednesdays from (correct date inserted for 2nd Wednesday of next month)

Exercise Con1b

Ref PC/WP/CON1B

(Date of typing)

FOR THE ATTENTION OF THE SPEAKER'S SECRETARY

Greenbank Centre
Greenbank Lane
DERBY
DE6 7JL

Dear Sirs

<u>WINE-MAKING</u>

I was pleased to receive your request for a presentation on the above topic which I think would be of interest to members of your organisation. A synopsis is given below.

<u>SYNOPSIS OF PRESENTATION</u>

A wide range of everyday things can be turned into wine and the results are often very palatable and cheap to produce. Berries, flowers, vegetables, fruits, leaves and weeds can all be transformed into interesting and colourful drinks.

Many suitable ingredients can be found in your garden (or in someone else's) so it is not always necessary to visit the greengrocer. You don't need to spend a lot of money on equipment and there are many shops and supermarkets offering everything you will need. However, you must always take great care in hygiene just as you would if you were preparing food.

Available Wednesdays from (correct date inserted for 2nd Wednesday of next month)

I would be obliged if you could let me know the date you would prefer as soon as possible as I have other organisations regularly contacting me, and I need a certain amount of time to make sure that I have a sufficiently wide range of wines to bring along to a demonstration.

A special feature of my talk is the opportunity to taste the different wines as well as being able to take away a copy of the easiest recipes. I will supply the wine if you will supply the glasses! I enclose one copy of my Recipes sheet which you are welcome to photocopy as necessary.

Exercise Con1b

My talk usually lasts for about one hour, followed by approximately half an hour for tasting and questions. I could be at your Centre at 1830 hours. If the talk began at 1900 hours, I would anticipate leaving at approximately 2100 hours. I do not charge a fee but would be obliged if you could let me have the token sum of £5 to cover expenses.

There are some items of wine-making equipment which I would like to show you, and I would need a large table to accommodate these.

Perhaps you could let me have directions and a map if possible to help me to find the Greenbank Centre. It would also be of great assistance to me if you could let me know where I can park my car when I arrive. There is quite a lot of carrying to be done both before and after the presentation so the nearer I can get to the Centre, the better.

I look forward to hearing from you.

Yours faithfully

PENNY CROFTON (MRS)

Enc

Exercise Con1c

WINES FROM YOUR GARDEN

C O U N T R Y   W I N E - M A K I N G

A wide range of everyday things can be turned into wine and the results are often very palatable and cheap to produce. Berries, flowers, vegetables, fruits, weeds and leaves can all be transformed into interesting and colourful drinks.

Many suitable ingredients can be found in your garden (or in someone else's) so it is not always necessary to visit the greengrocer. You don't need to spend a lot of money on equipment and there are many shops and supermarkets offering everything you will need.

1

Exercise Con1c

WINES FROM YOUR GARDEN

<u>BASIC FACTS</u>

During my talk you had the opportunity to taste the different wines. My Recipes sheet gives some easy recipes.

The main stages of country wine-making are:

1 Extraction of flavour and colour

2 Addition of other ingredients and fermenting

3 Straining

4 Fermenting

5 Racking

6 Bottling

7 Storing - for at least six months

The main ingredient is the fruit, vegetables, flowers or herbs which give the wine its individual colour, taste and smell.

Yeast is the most important ingredient in country wine-making - it must be wine yeast - and a yeast nutrient should be added.

Sugar must be carefully weighed before it is made into a syrup, ie dissolved in hot water, and added to the 'must'.

2

Exercise Con1c

WINES FROM YOUR GARDEN

<u>WINE-MAKING EQUIPMENT</u>

It is not necessary to spend a lot of money on special equipment. You probably have most things in your kitchen already. However, you must always take great care in hygiene just as you would if you were preparing food.

Many supermarkets have a range of country wine-making equipment and there are specialist shops for the enthusiast. Perhaps one of the most helpful aids is your cellar book where you can record details of each wine. You can have great fun, if you have artistic leanings, in designing your own labels.

Any kind of bottle will do for your wine provided it is a <u>wine</u> bottle. Restaurants are usually happy to give away their empties. You will also need:

corks
bottle brush
siphon hose
corking tool
straining cloths

A wide range of everyday things can be turned into wine and the results are often very palatable and cheap to produce.

3

Unit 4

Exercise 4c

```
                    BRITANNIA BULBS ORDER FORM
                          26 Rocks Road
                            Sheffield
                             S4 7JB

Customer Name: Mrs J Smithies
Address: Woodnook Cottage
         Woodnook Close
         BRADFORD
Post Code: BD5 TR2             Tel No: 0274 384572

Bulbs Type: Tulips
Variety: Queen Alicia
Cat No: TU3782
Quantity: 3 dozen
Price: £2.35 per dozen
Date of Order: 15 July 1992
Method of Payment: Cheque

-------------------------------------------------------
TO BE COMPLETED BY DESPATCH DEPARTMENT

Despatch Date ................ Despatched by ...............
```

Exercise 4d

```
                    BRITANNIA BULBS ORDER FORM
                          26 Rocks Road
                            Sheffield
                             S4 7JB

Customer Name: Walter Riley
Address: 4 Bridge Lane
         HUDDERSFIELD
Post Code: HD2 FL8             Tel No: 0484 37625

Bulbs Type: Crocus
Variety: Mixed
Cat No: CR2212
Quantity: 5 dozen
Price: £1.50 per dozen
Date of Order: 16 July 1992
Method of Payment: Visa
-------------------------------------------------------------
TO BE COMPLETED BY DESPATCH DEPARTMENT

Despatch Date ................ Despatch Date ................
```

Exercise 4e

W H BRIDGES & CO
SALES PROMOTION - WEEKEND RESIDENTIAL

PERSONNEL ACCOMMODATION DETAILS

Branch: LEEDS   Branch No: 346

Branch Tel No: 0532 683462

No of Personnel attending: 2
Name(s) of Personnel: Chris Blanchard
                      Diane Whitely

Date of Residential: From: 2 August 1992   To: 3 August 1992
Accommodation required: 2 single rooms with bath

Attendance confirmed on (date): 27 July 1992

Unit 5

Exercise 5b

BRITANNIA BULBS
26 Rocks Road
Sheffield
S4 7JB

Tel No: 0742 472831

(today's date)

Mrs J Smithies
Woodnook Cottage
Woodnook Close
BRADFORD BD5 2TR

Dear Mrs Smithies

RE YOUR ORDER OF 15 JULY 1992

Thank you for your recent order for a selection of our bulbs.

Our records show your order was for: 3 dozen Tulips, Queen Alicia variety at a cost of £2.35 per dozen.

We are pleased to advise you that these items are in stock and should arrive within the next fourteen days.

A receipt for your cheque will be enclosed with the bulbs, along with instructions for planting.

We look forward to hearing from you again.

Yours sincerely
BRITTANIA BULBS

Sales Department

Exercise 5c

BRITANNIA BULBS
26 Rocks Road
Sheffield
S4 7JB

Tel No: 0742 472831

(today's date)

Mr Walter Riley
4 Bridge Lane
HUDDERSFIELD
HD2 8FL

Dear Mr Riley

Thank you for your recent order for a selection of our bulbs.

Our records show that your order was for 5 dozen Mixed Crocus bulbs, Cat No CR2212, and that you have already paid in full by VISA.

We are sorry to advise you that these items are currently out of stock. In fact, your order was taken from a catalogue which was out-of-date. Please find enclosed an up-to-date price list and this season's brochure.

We will be pleased to supply you with an alternative selection from the new catalogue or offer you a full refund. Please accept our apologies for any inconvenience caused, **along with the attached 50p voucher.**

Yours sincerely
BRITTANIA BULBS

Sales Department

Encs

Exercise 5d

BRITANNIA BULBS
26 Rocks Road
Sheffield
S4 7JB

Tel No: 0742 472831

(today's date)

H Jones & Son
Beaver Works
Drye Road
HALIFAX
HX4 8UY

Dear Sirs

Thank you for your recent enquiry regarding a selection of our bulbs.

We are pleased to hear of your intentions to improve the firm's car-parking area with bulbs and shrubbery, and would like to take this opportunity to tell you about our new **Garden Helpline Service**.

Details of this are explained in the accompanying leaflet, along with our new **Gardener's Helpline Telephone Number**.

When returning your order form, could you please let us know where you saw our advertisement as this will assist our marketing department.

Please find enclosed an up-to-date price list and this season's brochure.

Yours faithfully
BRITTANIA BULBS

Sales Department

Encs

Unit 6

Exercise 6b

BRITTANIA BULBS

LATEST ADDITIONS TO THE CATALOGUE:

BULB DESCRIPTION	CAT NO	PRICE	UNIT
SPRING FLOWERING			
CROCUS - Purple Delight	CR2213	£1.65	dozen
IRIS - Lilac Lady	IRI21	£2.40	dozen
TULIP - Princess Orange Maiden . . .	TU3784	£3.50	dozen
ANENOME - Rainbow Palette	AN8167	£4.55	fifty
SPECIAL SPRING MIXTURE*	SB14	£10.00	hundred
AUTUMN FLOWERING			
ZEPHYRANTHES - Autumn Breeze	ZE13	£0.45	each
GLADIOLUS - White Heat	GL36	£0.75	three
ACIDANTHERA - Princess Rhia	AC3334	£0.95	each
SPECIAL AUTUMN MIXTURE	SB14	£15.00	hundred

* Also available in Units of 500 at a Discount Price of £35.00

Exercise 6c

W H BRIDGES & CO SALES PROMOTION

WEEKEND RESIDENTIAL

The following personnel are to be directly involved with the company's new sales promotion scheme. Their names need to be added to the attendance list for the **weekend residentials** to be held in August.

BRANCH	BRANCH NAME	PAYROLL NO	NAME	DATE OF W/R*
311	BRADFORD	37268	ASHRAF AKBAR	10/8/92
237	YORK	27346	SUSANNAH BLAKELY	17/8/92
346	LEEDS	23672	CHRIS BLANCHARD	3/8/92
237	YORK	18384	CHRISTOPHER BLAND	17/8/92
119	HUDDERSFIELD	27474	MARTIN HOLROYD	24/8/92
119	HUDDERSFIELD	36272	STEPHEN ITRYCH	24/9/92
314	SHEFFIELD	37283	MAVIS RAWSON	10/8/92
311	BRADFORD	28473	MARGARET SUNCLIFFE	10/8/92
346	LEEDS	24671	DIANE WHITELY	3/8/92

* The **Weekend Residentials** start on the dates listed in the table above but a number of personnel will require an overnight stay the previous night - details of these to follow shortly.

Exercise 6d

MUSIC PROMOTIONS LTD

SPECIAL OFFERS

We are pleased to announce this month's special offers. All units are supplied in black ash effect finish. Special discounts are available on bulk orders (25 or more).

ITEM DESCRIPTION	SIZE	CAT NO	PRICE
DEXCEL 2-drawer compact disc storage unit	12x12x7 in	WR114	5.25
NEWSTYLE cassette carousel	7x7x10 in	ZX727	3.99
REGENT 3-drawer audio cassette storage cabinet	14x12x7 in	ZX235	14.99
STAVER 4-drawer compact disc library cabinet	13x5x16 in	WR256	12.99
XENON de-luxe audio cassette storage case*	7x7x11 in	ZX551	5.49

* This item also available in luxury, green leather-look vinyl.

Consolidation 2

Exercise Con2b

THE THREE EAGLES HOTEL

WEDDING RECEPTION BOOKING FORM

NAME Susan Bailey
ADDRESS 2 Grandsmere Place, Manchester
TEL NO 061-4782001

NO OF GUESTS 150	ROOM REQUIRED Atlantic
RECEPTION DATE September 12	RECEPTION TIME 1.30 pm - 4.30 pm

TYPE OF CATERING REQUIRED
Carvery

COST OF ROOM £55.00	COST OF CATERING (per head) £7.50
DEPOSIT PAID £50.00	DATE 18 July

Exercise Con2d

THE THREE EAGLES HOTEL
4 Grandways Road
MANCHESTER MN4 ET2

(today's date)

Miss Susan Bailey
2 Grandsmere Place
MANCHESTER

Dear Susan

WEDDING RECEPTION

I am pleased to confirm the provisional booking for your wedding reception to take place on 12 September.

CATERING

I believe you have requested CARVERY-style catering @ £7.50 per head. As an alternative, you may wish to consider our hot and cold Buffet menus. Please find enclosed some sample menus of all our catering options.

ROOM

You have been allocated the ATLANTIC ROOM which will comfortably hold between 125-160 guests and will therefore accommodate your present guest list.

A fixed charge of £55 is payable for the room. Should you find you need to cater for additional guests, we can offer a larger room at no extra cost providing you notify us within the next month.

ACCOMMODATION

I understand you have relatives attending the function who wish to book an overnight stay at the Hotel. Please send us details of any requirements as soon as possible.

I shall contact you again in due course to make final arrangements.

Best wishes

Jane Lumb (MANAGERESS)

Encs

Exercise Con2e

THE THREE EAGLES
4 Grandways Road
MANCHESTER MN4 ET2

FUNCTION BOOKINGS - SEPTEMBER

Hotel rooms have been booked for the following dates in September. Please arrange for temporary staff to be contracted for all events, but particularly where there are high guest numbers.

CLIENT NAME	MENU	COST ( ) PER HEAD	GUEST NOS	DATE BOOKED
Margaret Helm	CARVERY	£7.50	100	2 SEP
Mohammed Zafar	HOT BUFFET	£6.50	125	8 SEP
Susan Bailey	CARVERY	£7.50	155	12 SEP
Anabella Ferrybridge	HOT BUFFET	£6.50	60	13 SEP
Henry Swan	CHEESE/WINE	£4.75*	50	18 SEP
David Ridgeway	COLD BUFFET	£5.50	85	20 SEP
Sebastian MacIntosh	COLD BUFFET	£5.50	100	22 SEP
Betty Walsden	CARVERY	£7.50	145	26 SEP

* Cost per head conditional on available house wines.

Allocate space

six clear lines = 1 in
10 characters = 1 in (10 pitch)
12 characters = 1 in (12 pitch)
Note: remember to change right margin to allocate space at right of document

Bold text

Press: **F6** (to *start* bold)
Type: **text to be emboldened**
Press: **F6** again (to *end* bold)

Font / Appearance / Bold

To embolden text already keyed in

Press: **F12** or **Alt** + **F4**

Edit / Block

Shade area of text to be emboldened
Press: **F6**

Font / Appearance / Bold

To remove bold

See *Remove text emphasis*

Blocked capitals

Press: **caps lock key**

Case, to switch upper and lower

Shade block of text to be changed with **F12** or **Alt** + **F4**

Edit / Block

Press: **Shift** + **F3**
Select: **1** (Upper case) or **2** (Lower case)

Edit / Convert / Case

Centre text

Press: **Shift** + **F6**
(cursor jumps to centre of line)
Type: **text to be centred**
Press: ↵ (text is centred)

Layout / Justify / Centre

To centre text already keyed in

Press: **F12** or **Alt** + **F4**

Edit / Block

Shade area of text to be centred
Press: **Shift** + **F6**
Answer **[Cntr]? Y/N** with **Y**(es)

Layout / Justify / Centre

To remove centring

See *Remove text emphasis*

To centre a page top to bottom

Press: **Shift** + **F8**
Select: **2** (Page) **1** (Centre Page) **Y**(es)

Layout / Page

Change logged drive

Press: **F5**
Type: =A: ↵ (or specify drive letter required)
Press: **F1**

Clear screen

Press: **F7** **N** (No) **N** (No)

Copy text

Press: **F12** or **Alt** + **F4**

Edit / Block

Shade area of text to be copied
Press: **Ctrl** + **F4**
Press: **1** (Block) **2** (Copy)

Edit / Copy

Position cursor where text is to be copied *to*
Press: ↵

Cursor movement

Around document

Press: ← → ↑ ↓

Word by word

Press: **Ctrl** + ← or **Ctrl** + →

Start/end of line

Press: Home + ← or Home + →

End of screen

Press: Home ↓

Start of screen

Press: Home ↑

End of document

Press: Home Home ↓

Start of document

Press: Home Home ↑

To move cursor to a specified page

Press: **Ctrl** + **Home**
Type: **no of page required <**

Date command

Press: **Shift** + **F5**

Tools / Date / Format

To set date format

Press: **3**
Type: **1 3 4** (i.e. format as 1 January 1992)

To insert date at cursor:

Press: **1**

Tools / Date / Text

Delete a character

Move cursor to incorrect character
Press: **Del**
or
Move cursor to right of incorrect character
Press: ← (Del)

Delete to end of line

Press: **Ctrl** + **End**

Delete to end of sentence

Move cursor to start of sentence
Press: **F12** or **Alt** + **F4**
Press: **.** (full stop)
Press: **Del**
Type: **Y** (for Yes)

Edit / Select / Sentence / Delete

Delete to end of page

Press: **Ctrl** + **PgDn**
Press: **Y** (for Yes)

Edit / Select / Page / Delete

Delete a word

Move cursor to incorrect word
Press: **Ctrl** + ← (Del)

Delete a paragraph

Move cursor to beginning of paragraph (Block of text)
Press: **F12** or **Alt** + **F4**
Shade area of text to delete
Press: **Del**
Type: **Y** (for Yes)

Edit / Select / Paragraph / Delete

Entry points

To set up

Use a suitable symbol for the entry point which doesn't normally appear in the text, e.g. **$** or @.

To search for

Operate *Search* command (**F2**) to locate the entry point. Delete it, then replace with appropriate information.

Search / Forward

(Use *Typeover* mode if there is more than one entry point on the line.)
Note: remember to align entry points with a tab setting for information going on to more than one line

Exit WordPerfect

Press: **F7**

File
Exit

Type: **Y** (Yes) or **N** (No)
(to save file before exiting)
Type: **Y** (to exit)

Flush right text

Press: **Alt** + **F6**

Layout
Justify
Right

(cursor jumps to right margin)
Type: **text to be right aligned**
Press: ↵

Footers

Position cursor at top of document, but after any header command
Press: **Shift** + **F8** (format menu)

Layout
Page

Select: **2** (Page) **4** (Footer)
1 (Footer A)
Select: **2** (Every Page) (or choose another option)
Type: **the footer text**
Press: **F7** (exit footer screen)

Footer with automatic page numbering

Repeat as for entering a footer, but after entering the footer text (e.g. page no):
Press: **Ctrl** + **B** (**^B**)
Note: text is not vital, **^B** can be used alone

Footnotes

Manual method

Use asterisk(s) e.g. * ** *** or **superscripted number** ([3]) to enter footnote(s) in body of text (no space before footnote symbol)
Leave one space after explanatory footnote symbol(s) at bottom of passage/document

Headers

Position cursor at top of document
Press: **Shift** + **F8** (Format menu)

Layout
Page

Select: **2** (Page) **3** (Headers)
1 (Header A)
Select: **2** (Every Page) (or choose another option)
Type: **the header text**
Press: **F7** (exit header screen)

Help

For information on any of WordPerfect's functions
Press: **F3** (the help key)

Help

Press: **the first letter of the feature you require information on**
or
Press: **F3** again (to display the help template)
Press: **the feature function key for additional information**
Press: **space bar** or ↵ to exit help

Insert text

Simply type in character(s) at the appropriate place (making sure typeover mode is not in use)

Inset/indent key

Press: **F4** (to indent at left margin only)
Press: **Shift** + **F4** (to indent at left *and* right margins)

Layout
Align
Indent →
or
Indent →←

Note: Each time you press **F4** you indent by five spaces – press once to indent ($\frac{1}{2}$ in) – press twice to indent 1 in etc.

Justification on/off

Press: **Shift** + **F8**

Layout
Line
Justify
Full

Select: **1** (Line) **3** (Justification)
Version 5.0
Type: **Y** (Yes) or **N** (No)
Version 5.1
Type: **4** (Full) or **1** (Left)

Line length to alter

When using 10 pitch, 82 characters will fit on an A4 page. With default margins of 1 in, the line length is reduced to 62 characters.

To alter the line length to a specified setting, either add or subtract to the margin settings as appropriate (e.g. to set a line length of 52 you could change both margins to 15.

Line spacing

Press: **Shift** + **F8**

Layout
Line

Select: **1** (Line) **6** (Line Spacing)
Type: **1** (Single) **2** (Double)

Margins (to change)

Press: **Shift** + **F8**

Layout
Line

Select: **1** (Line) **7** (Margins)
Enter new left/right margin settings
Press: ↵ twice (to get back to document)

Margin release

Press: **Shift** + **Tab** to release the left margin temporarily

Marking files on List Files directory

From the List Files screen, position cursor on filename
Type: *
To mark all files
Press: **Home** *
To remove markers repeat procedure

Move block of text

Press: **F12** or **Alt** + **F4**

Edit
Block

Shade area of text to be moved
Press: **Ctrl** + **F4**

Edit
Move

Press: **1** (Block) **1** (Move)
Position cursor where text is to be moved to
Press: ↵

New page marker

Press: **Ctrl** + ↵

Layout
Align
Hard
Page

To delete a new page marker use reveal codes to position cursor on the code and press **Del**.

Page numbering

Position cursor at top of document, but after any header code
Press: **Shift** + **F8** (Format menu)

Layout
Page

Select: **2** (Page)
Version 5.0:
Select: **7** (Page Numbering)
Version 5.1:
Select: **6** (Page Numbering)
4 (Page Numbering position)
Select: **the number position required**
Press: **F7** (exit)
Press: **F7** (exit)

Suppress page numbering on current page

After selecting the number position:
Version 5.0
Select: **9** (Suppress this page only)
Version 5.1
Select: **8**
Select: **4** (Suppress Page Numbering)
Type: **Y** (for Yes)
Press: **F7** (exit)

Paragraphs

To make

Move cursor to first letter of new paragraph
Press: ↵ twice

To join

Move cursor to start of paragraph 2
Press: ←(Del) twice

Pitch, to change

Position cursor at top of document
Press: **Ctrl** + **F8**
Select: **4** (Base Font)
Select: **the required pitch**
(e.g. 12 CPI) by highlighting with cursor and pressing **1** (select)

Font / Base / Font

Print

Full document

Press: **Shift** + **F7**
Press: **1** (Full Document)

File / Print

One page

Position cursor on page to be printed
Press: **Shift** + **F7**
Press: **2** (Page)

File / Print

Print from List Files screen

Press: **F5** ↵ to bring up the List Files directory screen
Move cursor to highlight the file to print
Press: **4** (Print)
Press: **A**(ll) to print all pages in file
or key in number of page(s) to be printed (e.g. **3** to print page 3 only)

File / List Files

Remove text emphasis

Press: **F11** or **Alt** + **F3**
Using arrow keys to move cursor, shade the code to be deleted
(e.g. [**BOLD**], [**UND**], [**CNTR**])
Press: **Del** key
Press: **F11** or **Alt** + **F3** again
(to return to document)

Edit / Reveal Codes

Replace text – typeover

Move cursor to incorrect entry
Press: **Ins** key (typeover *on*)
Overtype with correct entry
Press: **Ins** key again (typeover *off*)

Restore deleted text

Press: **F1** (Cancel key)
Press: **1** (Restore last deletion) or
Press: **2** (Restore next to last deletion)

Edit / Undelete

Retrieve a file

Press: **F5**
(check you are on the right drive)
Select: **filename**
(use arrow keys to shade)
Press: **1** (Retrieve)
Y (Yes – if you are retrieving into your current file)
or
Press: **F10**
Type: **filename** ↵

File / List / Files

File / Retrieve

Save text and continue

Press: **F10**
Enter **your filename**
Note: type **Y**(Yes) if you want to *replace* a previous file with the same name

File / Save

Save text and exit

Press: **F7**
Type: **Y** (to save document)
Enter: **your filename**
Press: **Y** (to exit the program)

File / Save

Search for text

Press: **F2** (search forwards) or
Shift + **F2** (search backwards)
Key in text to search for
Press: **F2** (to begin search)
WordPerfect will search through the document and stop on the first occurrence of the 'search'
Press: **F2** again to continue the search

Search / Backwards

Search / Forwards

Search / Next

Search and replace

Position cursor at top of document
Press: **Alt** + **F2**
Press: **Y**(es) to confirm each replacement
or **N**(o) to replace without confirmation
Type the text (or enter the code) to be searched for
Press: **F2**
Type the replacement text (or replacement code)
Press: **F2**
Confirm where appropriate with **Y**(es)
'**Not found**' indicates end of search
Note: when searching/replacing a 'code' simply press the appropriate function key

Search / Replace

Search and replace 'beep'

To set a warning 'beep' for end of search
Press: **Shift** + **F1** (Set-up)
Version 5.0
Press: **5** (Initial Settings)
Version 5.1
Press: **3** (Environment)
Select: **Beep Options**
Press: **3** (Beep on Search Failure)
Press: **Y** (for Yes)
Press: **F7** (to exit this menu)

File / Setup / Environment

Sort, by line

Press: **F12** or **Alt** + **F4** and shade the portion of text to be sorted — Edit / Block
Press: **Ctrl** + **F9** — Tools / Sort
Select: **3** (Keys)
Select: **a**(lphanumeric) or **n**(umeric) to determine the type of sort
Enter: **the field number of your first sort key** (or press ↵ to accept 1)
Enter: **the word in the field to sort on** – **1**, **2**, **3**, etc (or press ↵ to accept 1)
Press: **F7** (exit definition area)
Press: **1** (Perform Action)

To sort in descending order

Repeat above procedure, but before pressing 1 perform action:
Select: **6** (Order) **2** (Descending)

Spaced capitals

Press: **caps lock** key
Leave *one space between each letter*
Leave *three spaces between each word*

Spellcheck

Press: **Ctrl** + **F2** — Tools / Spell
Select: **1 Word** (check word)
2 Page (check page)
3 Document (check document)
Select: **4 New sup. dictionary** (if the word is not already in WordPerfect's dictionary and you wish to add it in)
Select: **5 Look up** (to check a spelling you are not sure of e.g. typing cons* ↵ will bring up any word with the sequence cons)
Select: **Skip once** (to skip the word the first time it occurs but stop on it whenever it occurs again)
Skip (to skip the word on every occurrence)
Edit (to return to document and amend the error, then Press: **F7** to exit back to Speller)
Press: '**A**' (or the appropriate letter to select a correct spelling)
Press: **F7** (to return to document)

To spellcheck a block of text

Press: **F12** or **Alt** + **F4** and shade the area of text to be checked — Edit / Block
Press: **Ctrl** + **F2** — Tools / Spell
Continue with speller as normal

Standard paragraphs

Position cursor where you wish to insert the text
Retrieve the file
(see methods described under this heading)
Press: **PgDn** to go quickly to end of retrieved text

Tabulation

Default tabs

Press: **Tab** key
(to move cursor to defaulted tabs already pre-set every five spaces)

To alter tab settings at tab menu

Press: **Shift** + **F8** — Layout / Line
Select: **1** (Line) **8** (Tab Set)

To clear all tabs

Type: **0** (zero) (not necessary in Version 5.1)
Press: **Ctrl** + **End** key once
(All the 'Ls' (tab stops) should disappear)
Note: this is known as 'delete EOL' (Delete to End Of Line)

To delete one tab

Position cursor on tab to be deleted
Press: **Del** key

To set a tab

Position cursor on ruler line where tab is to be inserted
Press: **L** (left justified tab)
R (right justified tab)
C (centred tab)
D (decimal tab)
.+L or **.+R** (to display leader dots with a left or right tab setting)

To set tabs at regular intervals

Clear all tabs
Type: **0,5** (to set tabs every five spaces)
0,10 (to set tabs every ten spaces)

To exit tab menu

Press: **F7** twice
(to exit tab menu and return to document)
Note: pressing any other key, e.g. **F1** or **Esc** or ↵ will *not* save the changes

Underline text

Press: **F8** (to *start* underline) — Font / Appearance / Underline
Type: **text to be underlined**
Press: **F8** again (to *end* underline)

To underline text already keyed in

Press: **F12** or **Alt** + **F4**
Shade area of text to be underlined
Press: **F8** — Font / Appearance / Underline

To remove underline

See *remove text emphasis*

View document

Press: **Shift** + **F7** — File / Print
Press: **6** (View Document)
Select from options shown to see enlarged or reduced view of text
Press: **F7** to return to document
Note: use this option to view headers, footers, justification, footnotes, etc.

View file directory

Press: **F5** ← (List Files) — File / List Files

Widow/orphan protection

Position cursor at top of document
Press: **Shift** + **F8** (Format menu) — Layout / Line
Select: **1** (Line) **9** (**W/O** protection)
Type: **Y** (for Yes)
Press: **F7** (exit)

> **Important!**
> In WordPerfect there is no single 'panic' key (the key to press to go back a step or get you out of an option you selected by mistake)
> Generally, in order to:
> ***Cancel a command*** Press: **F1**
> ***Exit a 'menu'*** Press: **F7**